The Essential Google Ads Guide:

Unlock The Power of Google Ads

William Buck

TABLE OF CONTENTS

CHAPTER FOURTEEN: KEEPING UP WITH GOOGLE ADS UPDATES

A. Staying informed about Google Ads changes

B. Best practices for adapting to updates

CHAPTER FIFTEEN: CONCLUSION

OVERVIEW OF THE BOOK

Welcome to "The Essential Google Ads Guide" - your ultimate resource for unlocking the power of Google Ads and accelerating your business growth. In today's digital landscape, having a strong online presence is crucial, and Google Ads offers an unparalleled platform to connect with your target audience and drive meaningful conversions.

This comprehensive guide is meticulously crafted to provide you with a step-by-step roadmap, regardless of your level of experience with online advertising. Whether you're a small business owner looking to expand your reach or a seasoned marketer aiming to optimize your campaigns, this guide is designed to equip you with the knowledge and strategies necessary to succeed.

From the very beginning, you'll dive into the fundamentals of Google Ads, demystifying its interface and understanding its benefits. You'll learn how to create and structure your account effectively, ensuring a solid foundation for your advertising efforts. Keyword research and targeting will no longer be a mystery, as you discover the tools and techniques to identify the most relevant keywords for your business and optimize your campaigns accordingly.

Crafting compelling ad campaigns is an art, and this book provides you with the tools to master it. You'll uncover the secrets to writing persuasive ad copy that captures attention and drives clicks. Additionally, you'll explore the world of ad extensions, discovering how to enhance your ads with additional information and enticing features.

But it doesn't stop there. This book takes you deeper into the realm of ad optimization, uncovering the mysteries behind Quality Score and Ad Rank. You'll gain insights into bidding strategies, budgeting techniques, and ways to track and measure your campaign performance effectively. With a focus on data-driven decision-making, you'll have the power to continually refine and improve your advertising efforts.

Expanding beyond the basics, this book explores advanced strategies such as remarketing, audience targeting, and mobile advertising. You'll unlock the potential of display ads, tap into local markets, and leverage advanced targeting options to reach the right audience at the right time.

To ensure your success, troubleshooting tips and optimization techniques are provided, helping you navigate common challenges and maximize the effectiveness of your campaigns. And as the ever-evolving world of Google Ads continues to change, you'll discover how to stay informed and adapt to updates seamlessly, keeping your campaigns ahead of the curve.

"The Essential Google Ads Guide" is your companion on the path to advertising success. With its practical and actionable insights, it empowers you to harness the full potential of Google Ads, drive targeted traffic to your business, and achieve measurable results. Get ready to unlock new growth opportunities, connect with your audience on a deeper level, and propel your business to new heights with the power of Google Ads.

CHAPTER ONE: INTRODUCTION TO GOOGLE ADS

A. What is Google Ads?

Google Ads is an online advertising platform developed by Google that allows businesses to display their ads on Google's search engine results pages, as well as on other Google-owned platforms and partner websites. It is one of the most widely used advertising platforms on the internet.

Google Ads operates on a pay-per-click (PPC) model, which means that advertisers only pay when someone clicks on their ad. This makes it a cost-effective advertising solution as businesses only incur costs when there is actual engagement with their ads.

The platform offers a variety of ad formats to suit different advertising goals and target audiences. The most common ad format is the text ad, which appears as a headline, a couple of lines of ad copy, and a URL. Other ad formats include display ads, which are image-based ads that can be placed on websites within the Google Display Network, and video ads that can be shown on YouTube or across the Google Display Network.

Google Ads provides advertisers with extensive targeting options to reach their desired audience. Advertisers can target their ads based on keywords, location, language, device type, and even specific demographics and interests. This level of targeting precision helps businesses reach the right audience at the right time, increasing the chances of generating relevant clicks and conversions.

To create and manage Google Ads campaigns, advertisers use the Google Ads interface, where they set their advertising budget, create ad groups, select keywords, and define bidding strategies. The platform also provides various tools and features to track the performance of campaigns, such as conversion tracking, audience insights, and detailed reporting.

Google Ads operates on an auction-based system, where advertisers bid for ad placement and compete with other advertisers targeting similar keywords or audiences. The bid amount, along with factors like ad relevance and expected click-through rate, determines the ad's position on the search results page or other placements.

Overall, Google Ads is a powerful advertising platform that allows businesses of all sizes to reach a vast online audience and promote their products or services effectively. Its targeting options, flexibility, and measurement capabilities make it a popular choice for advertisers looking to increase their online visibility and drive relevant traffic to their websites.

B. Benefits of using Google Ads

Google Ads offers several benefits for businesses looking to increase their online visibility and drive targeted traffic to their websites. Here are some of the key benefits of using Google Ads:

➢ Wide Audience Reach: Google is the most popular search engine worldwide, with billions of searches conducted every day. By advertising on Google Ads, businesses can reach a vast audience and increase their brand exposure.

➢ Targeted Advertising: Google Ads allows businesses to target their ads based on various factors such as keywords, demographics, location, and device type. This precise targeting ensures that ads are shown to the right audience at the right time, increasing the chances of attracting relevant traffic and potential customers.

➢ Cost Control: Google Ads provides flexible budget options, allowing businesses to set a daily or monthly budget according to their advertising goals and financial capacity. Additionally, Google Ads operates on a pay-per-click (PPC) model, meaning you only pay when someone clicks on your ad. This cost control feature makes it suitable for businesses of all sizes, from startups to large enterprises.

➢ Measurable Results: Google Ads provides detailed performance metrics, giving businesses insights into their campaigns' effectiveness. Key performance indicators such as impressions, clicks, click-through rates (CTRs), conversions, and return on investment (ROI) can be tracked, allowing businesses to evaluate the success of their advertising efforts and make data-driven decisions.

➢ Ad Extensions: Google Ads offers various ad extensions that allow businesses to enhance their ads and provide additional information to potential customers. Ad extensions such as site links, call extensions, location extensions, and review extensions increase the visibility and relevance of ads, improving the chances of attracting clicks and conversions.

➢ Remarketing: Google Ads enables businesses to target users who have previously interacted with their website or shown interest in their products or services. By using remarketing campaigns, businesses can reconnect with these users and increase the likelihood of conversions, as they are already familiar with the brand.

➢ Mobile Advertising: With the increasing use of mobile devices, Google Ads provides mobile-specific ad formats and targeting options, allowing businesses to effectively reach users on smartphones and tablets. This mobile advertising capability is crucial in today's mobile-centric world, ensuring that businesses don't miss out on potential customers.

➤ Ad Testing and Optimization: Google Ads offers robust testing and optimization features, enabling businesses to experiment with different ad variations, keywords, and targeting options. By continuously testing and refining their ads, businesses can improve their campaign performance and maximize their advertising budget.

➤ Competitor Insights: Google Ads provides valuable insights into competitors' advertising strategies, including the keywords they target, ad copy they use, and the positions they bid for. This competitive intelligence allows businesses to adapt their own campaigns, stay ahead of the competition, and gain a competitive edge.

Overall, using Google Ads offers businesses the advantages of wide audience reach, targeted advertising, cost control, measurable results, ad extensions, remarketing, mobile advertising, ad testing and optimization, and competitor insights. By leveraging these benefits, businesses can effectively promote their products or services, drive relevant traffic, and achieve their marketing goals.

C. Understanding the Google Ads interface

The Google Ads interface is a powerful platform that allows advertisers to create, manage, and optimize their online advertising campaigns across the Google network. Understanding the interface is essential for effectively utilizing Google Ads to drive targeted traffic and achieve marketing goals.

Here's an extensive explanation of the key components and features of the Google Ads interface:

➢ Dashboard: The dashboard is the main hub where you'll find an overview of your account's performance. It provides key metrics, such as impressions, clicks, conversions, and cost data. You can customize the dashboard to display the information most relevant to your campaign goals.

➢ Campaigns: Google Ads organizes advertising efforts into campaigns. Each campaign focuses on a specific objective, such as promoting a product, driving website traffic, or increasing brand awareness. Within a campaign, you can create multiple ad groups and ads.

➢ Ad Groups: Ad groups are subdivisions within a campaign that house a set of related keywords, ads, and landing pages. Structuring your campaigns with well-organized ad groups allows for more targeted and relevant advertising.

➢ Keywords: Keywords are the search terms or phrases that trigger your ads to appear when users search on Google. Google Ads offers various keyword match types, including broad match, phrase match, exact match, and broad match modifier, allowing you to control how closely a user's search must match your selected keywords.

➢ Ads: Ads are the creative elements displayed to users when triggered by relevant keywords. Google Ads supports various ad formats, including text ads, image ads, responsive ads, and video ads. You can create compelling ad copy, headlines, and descriptions to engage users and encourage clicks.

➢ Ad Extensions: Ad extensions enhance your ads with additional information and options for users. Examples include sitelink extensions (additional links to specific pages on your website), call extensions (phone numbers to encourage direct calls), and location extensions (displaying your business address).

➢ Quality Score: Quality Score is a metric that measures the relevance and quality of your keywords, ads, and landing pages. It influences your ad position, ad rank, and cost-per-click (CPC). Maintaining a high-quality score can improve your ad performance and lower costs.

➢ Bidding: Bidding determines how much you are willing to pay for clicks or conversions. Google Ads offers various bidding strategies, such as manual CPC (cost-per-click), target CPA (cost-per-action), and target ROAS (return on ad spend). Each strategy has its own benefits and should align with your campaign goals.

➢ Auction Insights: Auction Insights provides competitive data on how your ads are performing compared to other advertisers competing in the same auctions. It offers valuable insights into impression share, average position, and overlap with competitors, helping you refine your bidding and campaign strategies.

➢ Reports: Google Ads offers robust reporting features to analyze and measure your campaign performance. You can generate reports on key metrics, segment data by various dimensions (time, device, location, etc.), and apply filters to gain valuable insights into your advertising efforts.

➢ Conversion Tracking: Conversion tracking allows you to measure the actions users take after clicking on your ads, such as purchases, form submissions, or app downloads. By setting up conversion tracking, you can assess the effectiveness of your campaigns and optimize them for better results.

➢ Optimization Tools: Google Ads provides a range of optimization tools, including automated bidding, smart campaigns, and recommendations based on machine

learning. These tools can help streamline campaign management and improve performance.

Understanding the Google Ads interface is crucial for effectively managing your campaigns, optimizing performance, and achieving your advertising goals. By familiarizing yourself with these key components and features, you can make informed decisions and maximize the success of your Google Ads campaigns.

CHAPTER TWO: SETTING UP A GOOGLE ADS ACCOUNT

A. Creating a Google Ads account

To create a Google Ads account, follow these steps:

> ➤ Go to the Google Ads website: Visit the Google Ads homepage by typing "Google Ads" into your web browser's search bar or directly accessing ads.google.com.

> ➤ Sign in with a Google account: If you already have a Google account, sign in with your existing credentials. If not, you'll need to create a new Google account by clicking on the "Start Now" button and following the instructions provided.

> ➤ Provide basic information: After signing in, you'll be prompted to enter some basic information about your business or organization, such as the country and time zone where your ads will be targeted.

> ➤ Set up your first campaign: Google Ads operates on a campaign-based structure. A campaign is a container that holds your ads, targeting settings, and budget. To create your first campaign, click on the "+ Campaign" button.

➢ Select a campaign goal: Google Ads offers different campaign goals, such as driving website traffic, increasing sales, or raising brand awareness. Choose the goal that aligns with your advertising objectives.

➢ Choose a campaign type: Select the campaign type that suits your needs. Common campaign types include Search Network, Display Network, Shopping, Video, or App promotion. Each type serves different ad formats and reaches different audiences.

➢ Configure campaign settings: Provide specific details about your campaign, such as campaign name, budget, bidding strategy, and start and end dates. You can also set targeting options, such as geographic locations, languages, and audience demographics.

➢ Create ad groups: Within your campaign, you'll need to create ad groups. Ad groups allow you to organize your ads and target specific keywords or themes. Each ad group will have its own set of keywords and ads.

➢ Create ads: Build your ads by writing compelling headlines, descriptions, and display URLs. Depending on the campaign type, you may also need to upload images or videos. Follow Google's guidelines to ensure compliance with their ad policies.

➤ Set up billing: To run ads, you'll need to set up your billing information. Provide your billing address and payment details. Google Ads offers various payment options, including credit card, bank transfer, or direct debit.

➤ Review and launch: Double-check all the campaign settings, ad copy, and targeting options to make sure everything is accurate. Once you're satisfied, click the "Launch" or "Submit" button to start running your ads.

After launching your campaign, monitor its performance regularly and make necessary optimizations. Google Ads provides comprehensive reporting and analytics tools to track impressions, clicks, conversions, and other key metrics. Use this data to refine your campaigns and improve their effectiveness.

Remember, creating a successful Google Ads account requires continuous experimentation, testing, and optimization to achieve your advertising goals.

B. Understanding account structure and hierarchy

Google Ads account structure and hierarchy refer to the way campaigns, ad groups, and ads are organized within an account. Understanding this structure is essential for effectively managing and optimizing your Google Ads campaigns.

Let's delve into each level of the hierarchy and its purpose:

> Account: At the highest level, you have the Google Ads account. This is where you manage all your campaigns and associated settings. An account represents your overall advertising entity, whether it's a business, organization, or individual.

> Campaign: Within an account, you can create multiple campaigns. Each campaign should have a specific goal or objective, such as promoting a particular product or targeting a specific audience. Campaigns act as containers for your ads, keywords, and budget settings. Additionally, each campaign is a separate advertising initiative with its own budget, targeting settings, and campaign type. You can create multiple campaigns based on different objectives, such as promoting specific products or services, targeting different geographic locations, or focusing on various marketing strategies.

➢ Ad Group: Inside each campaign, you have ad groups. Ad groups serve as subcategories or themes within a campaign. They contain a set of related keywords, ads, and landing pages. Ad groups enable you to organize your ads based on common themes, allowing for better targeting and optimization. They help you organize your advertising efforts and maintain relevancy between keywords, ads, and landing pages.

➢ Ads: Within each ad group, you create individual ads. These ads are the actual content that users see when they search on Google or visit websites within the Google Display Network. You can create different types of ads, such as text ads, image ads, video ads, or responsive ads. Each ad should be tailored to resonate with your target audience and entice them to take the desired action. Additionally, ads consist of headlines, descriptions, display URLs, and other elements that communicate your message to potential customers. It's important to create compelling and persuasive ad copy that entices users to click on your ads and visit your website.

➢ Keywords: Keywords are a fundamental component of Google Ads. They are words or phrases that you choose to trigger the display of your ads when users search for those terms on Google. By selecting relevant keywords, you can reach your target audience effectively. Keywords are assigned at the ad group level and help determine when your ads are shown.

The hierarchy in Google Ads is designed to provide a logical structure that allows you to manage and optimize your campaigns efficiently. It offers flexibility in terms of budget allocation, targeting, and performance monitoring. Here are a few key benefits of understanding and utilizing the account structure:

➢ Organization and control: The hierarchical structure allows you to organize your campaigns, ad groups, and ads based on your business objectives, product lines, or target audiences. This organization makes it easier to manage and track performance at each level.

➢ Targeting and relevance: By grouping related keywords and ads into specific ad groups, you can create highly targeted campaigns. This helps ensure that your ads are relevant to users' search queries, which can improve click-through rates and conversion rates.

➢ Budget allocation: Google Ads provides you with the flexibility to allocate budgets at the campaign level. This means you can assign different budget amounts to different campaigns based on their importance or performance goals. It enables you to control your spending and prioritize campaigns accordingly.

➤ Performance monitoring and optimization: The account structure allows you to monitor the performance of each campaign, ad group, and ad individually. By analyzing metrics like impressions, clicks, click-through rates, and conversions, you can identify areas for improvement and optimize your campaigns to achieve better results.

Overall, understanding the Google Ads account structure and hierarchy is crucial for effectively organizing and managing your advertising campaigns. It helps you achieve better targeting, relevance, and control over your budget. By utilizing this structure and regularly optimizing your campaigns, you can maximize the performance and return on investment of your Google Ads efforts.

C. Account settings and preferences

Google Ads account settings and preferences are essential elements in optimizing your advertising campaigns and ensuring they align with your business goals. These settings allow you to customize various aspects of your Google Ads account to maximize your advertising performance. Let's explore some of the key settings and preferences available:

➤ **Account-level settings:** These settings apply to your entire Google Ads account and include options such as:

a. Time zone and currency: Specify the time zone and currency for your account to ensure accurate reporting and billing.

b. Billing settings: Set up your preferred payment methods, billing thresholds, and invoicing preferences.

c. Account access: Manage user access and permissions, granting different levels of account control to team members or agencies.

> **Campaign-level settings**:

These settings are specific to individual campaigns and allow you to fine-tune your advertising strategy. Some important options include:

a. Campaign type and subtype: Choose the appropriate campaign type based on your advertising objectives, such as Search, Display, Video, Shopping, or App.

b. Networks and devices: Select the networks (Search, Display, or both) where your ads will appear and specify device targeting preferences (desktop, mobile, tablet).

c. Bidding and budget: Define your bidding strategy (e.g., manual CPC, automated bidding) and set campaign budgets to control your spending.

d. Ad extensions: Enable various ad extensions, such as sitelinks, call extensions, or location extensions, to enhance your ad's visibility and engagement.

e. Ad scheduling: Determine when your ads will be shown by setting specific days and hours or adjusting bids based on time of day or day of the week.

★ **Ad group-level settings:**

These settings allow you to further optimize your advertising at a granular level within each campaign. Notable options include:

a. Ad rotation: Choose how your ads rotate within an ad group, such as evenly, optimized for clicks, or optimized for conversions.

b. Keyword matching options: Specify the match types for your keywords (e.g., broad match, phrase match, exact match) to control the relevance of your ad placements.

c. Audience targeting: Utilize audience targeting to reach specific groups of users based on demographics, interests, or remarketing lists.

d. Ad scheduling: Adjust bidding or ad visibility based on specific times or days within an ad group.

➤ **Other settings and preferences**:

Google Ads offers additional settings and preferences to enhance your advertising effectiveness, including:

a. Conversion tracking: Set up conversion tracking to measure the success of your campaigns and optimize for specific actions on your website.

b. Location targeting: Specify geographic locations where you want your ads to be shown, whether at the country, city, or radius level.

c. Language targeting: Define the languages in which your ads should be displayed to ensure they reach the relevant audience.

d. Ad delivery: Choose whether to optimize for clicks or conversions, or use accelerated delivery to show your ads as quickly as possible.

e. Exclusion settings: Exclude specific audiences, locations, or websites where you don't want your ads to appear.

By understanding and leveraging these Google Ads account settings and preferences, you can tailor your advertising campaigns to your business needs, reach the right audience, and maximize the return on your advertising investment.

CHAPTER THREE: KEYWORD RESEARCH AND TARGETING

A. Importance of keyword research

Keyword research is crucial in Google Ads campaigns because it helps advertisers understand the language and terms that their target audience uses when searching for products or services online. By conducting thorough keyword research, advertisers can identify and select relevant keywords that are most likely to attract qualified traffic to their website.

Here are several key reasons why keyword research is important in Google Ads:

➤ Targeted Advertising: Keyword research allows advertisers to specifically target their ads to users who are actively searching for their offerings. By selecting the right keywords, advertisers can ensure that their ads are displayed to an audience that is most likely to convert into customers. This helps maximize the return on investment (ROI) for advertising spend.

➤ Cost Efficiency: Keyword research helps advertisers identify relevant keywords with a reasonable level of search volume and relatively low competition. By targeting these keywords, advertisers can achieve a better ad position at a lower cost per click (CPC). This enables them to optimize their advertising budget and maximize their ad impressions and clicks.

➤ Ad Relevance: Selecting appropriate keywords ensures that the ads displayed to users align with their search queries. When ads are relevant to user intent, they are more likely to attract clicks, improve click-through rates (CTR), and enhance the overall quality score of the campaign. A higher quality score can lead to better ad rankings and lower costs.

➤ Expansion Opportunities: Keyword research not only helps advertisers identify the most relevant keywords but also provides insights into related keywords and search trends. By exploring these expansion opportunities, advertisers can broaden their reach and target a larger audience base. This allows them to tap into new markets and discover untapped potential for their products or services.

➤ Ad Copy and Landing Page Optimization: Keyword research also plays a significant role in creating compelling ad copy and optimizing landing pages. By understanding the keywords that resonate with their target audience, advertisers can tailor their ad messaging and landing page content to match user expectations. This leads to improved relevance, higher conversion rates, and a better user experience.

➢ Negative Keywords: In addition to selecting relevant keywords, keyword research helps identify negative keywords, which are search terms that are irrelevant to the advertiser's offerings. By including negative keywords in campaigns, advertisers can prevent their ads from being displayed to users who are unlikely to convert. This further improves ad targeting, reduces wasted ad spend, and enhances campaign efficiency.

B. Tools for keyword research

Keyword research is a critical aspect of successful Google Ads campaigns. It involves identifying the most relevant and effective keywords that potential customers are likely to use when searching for products or services. To help advertisers conduct thorough keyword research, several tools are available. Here are some of the most widely used tools for keyword research:

➢ Google Keyword Planner: This is a free tool provided by Google Ads. It allows advertisers to explore keyword ideas and estimate their search volume and competition levels. It provides valuable insights such as average monthly searches, competition levels, and suggested bid ranges. Additionally, it can generate keyword ideas based on a website or specific keywords.

➤ SEMrush: SEMrush is a comprehensive SEO and marketing tool that offers a robust keyword research feature. It provides data on keyword volume, keyword difficulty, and competition level. SEMrush also offers additional features like competitor analysis, backlink analysis, and rank tracking, making it a valuable tool for holistic marketing research.

➤ Ahrefs: Ahrefs is primarily known for its backlink analysis capabilities, but it also offers a powerful keyword research tool. It provides keyword data such as search volume, keyword difficulty, and keyword ideas. Ahrefs also offers advanced features like content gap analysis, where it suggests keywords that competitors are ranking for but you aren't, helping you identify untapped opportunities.

➤ Moz Keyword Explorer: Moz's Keyword Explorer provides valuable insights into keyword search volume, difficulty, and opportunity. It uses a unique metric called "Keyword Difficulty" to estimate how hard it would be to rank for a specific keyword. Moz also offers features like SERP analysis, where it shows the top-ranking pages for a given keyword and provides suggestions for related keywords.

➢ KeywordTool.io: This tool is useful for generating keyword ideas based on specific topics or seed keywords. It provides keyword suggestions for Google, Bing, YouTube, Amazon, and other search engines. KeywordTool.io also offers data on search volume, cost-per-click (CPC), and competition level for each keyword.

➢ Ubersuggest: Ubersuggest, created by Neil Patel, offers an intuitive interface for keyword research. It provides keyword suggestions, search volume, CPC, and competition data. Ubersuggest also offers features like domain analysis and content ideas, making it a comprehensive SEO tool.

These tools can significantly streamline the keyword research process by providing valuable data and insights. However, it's important to note that no tool can guarantee the success of a Google Ads campaign. Effective keyword research requires a combination of tool analysis, market knowledge, and continuous optimization based on campaign performance.

C. Types of keyword match types

There are three primary types of keyword match types in Google Ads: broad match, phrase match, and exact match. Each match type determines how closely a user's search query must match your keywords for your ad to be eligible to appear.

> ➢ Broad Match: This is the default match type and offers the widest reach. With broad match, your ads may appear for variations, synonyms, misspellings, and related searches, as well as for searches Google considers relevant. For example, if your keyword is "women's shoes," your ad might show up for searches like "ladies' footwear" or "shoes for women." While broad match provides broad visibility, it can also lead to irrelevant clicks, so it's important to regularly review and refine your keyword list to optimize performance.

> ➢ Phrase Match: This match type provides more control than broad match while still reaching a broader audience than exact match. When using phrase match, your ad will appear when someone's search query contains the exact phrase or a close variation of it. The order of the words must remain intact, but there may be additional words before or after the phrase. For example, if your keyword is "red shoes," your ad may be triggered by searches like "buy red shoes" or "red shoes for sale." However, it will not show for searches like "shoes that are red."

➢ Exact Match: This match type offers the most precise targeting. Your ad will only appear when someone searches for your keyword or a close variation of it without any additional words before or after the keyword. Exact match ensures a higher degree of relevance and reduces the likelihood of irrelevant clicks. For instance, if your keyword is [running shoes], your ad might show for searches like "running shoes" but not for "best running shoes" or "shoes for running."

Additionally, there are two additional match types worth mentioning:

➢ Broad Match Modifier (BMM): BMM allows you to specify certain words that must be present in the user's search query for your ad to appear. By adding a plus symbol (+) in front of these words, you create a modified broad match. This match type offers more control than broad match while maintaining a broad reach. For example, if your BMM keyword is +running +shoes, your ad could show for searches like "best running shoes" or "buy running shoes."

➢ Negative Match: Negative keywords are used to prevent your ads from showing for certain search terms. By specifying negative keywords, you can exclude irrelevant searches and avoid wasting ad spend. For example, if you sell new shoes, you can add the negative keyword "used" to prevent your ad from appearing for searches like "used shoes."

Choosing the right match type depends on your advertising goals, target audience, and the level of control you want over the search terms triggering your ads. A combination of match types is often recommended to strike a balance between reach and relevance while maximizing the effectiveness of your Google Ads campaigns.

D. Refining keyword targeting

Refining keyword targeting is a crucial aspect of optimizing Google Ads campaigns to maximize their effectiveness. By narrowing down and refining the keywords you target, you can increase the relevance of your ads and improve their performance. Here are some key points to consider when refining keyword targeting:

> ➤ Keyword Research: Start by conducting thorough keyword research to identify the most relevant keywords for your business. Use tools like Google Keyword Planner, SEMrush, or Moz Keyword Explorer to discover relevant keywords with high search volume and low competition.

> ➤ Keyword Match Types: Google Ads offers different keyword match types that determine how closely a user's search query must match your targeted keyword for your

ad to be triggered. The match types include broad match, broad match modifier, phrase match, and exact match. Each match type has its pros and cons, and using a combination of match types can help you refine your targeting.

➤ Negative Keywords: Negative keywords are search terms you specify to prevent your ads from showing for irrelevant searches. By adding negative keywords, you can exclude unrelated queries and focus your ads on the most relevant audience. Regularly review your search terms report and identify irrelevant search queries to add them as negative keywords.

➤ Geographic Targeting: Refine your keyword targeting by narrowing down your ads' visibility to specific geographic locations. If your business operates in certain regions or cities, consider targeting keywords specific to those locations or exclude locations where you don't provide services.

➤ Ad Group Structure: Organize your keywords into tightly themed ad groups to ensure your ads are highly relevant to the search queries triggered. Grouping related keywords together allows you to create more targeted ad copy and landing pages, leading to higher click-through rates (CTRs) and better ad performance.

➢ Quality Score Optimization: Google's Quality Score measures the relevance of your keywords, ad copy, and landing pages. By optimizing these elements and increasing your Quality Score, you can improve your ad position and lower your cost per click (CPC). Ensure your keywords are closely aligned with your ad text and landing page content to boost your Quality Score.

➢ Regular Monitoring and Optimization: Refining keyword targeting is an ongoing process. Continuously monitor your campaign's performance, review search term reports, and identify new keyword opportunities or negative keywords. Test different variations of keywords, match types, and ad copy to identify what works best for your campaign.

Remember, refining keyword targeting is not a one-time task. It requires ongoing analysis, optimization, and adaptation to stay competitive in the dynamic online advertising landscape. By continually refining your keyword targeting, you can improve the relevance of your ads, increase click-through rates, and ultimately drive more conversions for your business.

CHAPTER FOUR: CREATING EFFECTIVE AD CAMPAIGNS

A. Campaign types and goals

Google Ads offers several campaign types and goals to help advertisers reach their marketing objectives. Let's explore each campaign type and its associated goals:

I. Search Campaigns:

- Goal: Drive relevant traffic by displaying text ads in Google search results when users search for specific keywords related to your products or services.
- Reach: Reach potential customers actively searching for your offerings.
- Ad Format: Text-based ads with headlines, descriptions, and display URLs.

II. Display Campaigns:

- Goal: Increase brand awareness and reach a wider audience by showing image or video ads on websites within the Google Display Network (GDN).
- Reach: Display ads across millions of websites, mobile apps, and YouTube videos.
- Ad Format: Image or video ads in various sizes and formats.

III. Video Campaigns:

Goal: Engage users with video content and drive actions such as views, clicks, or conversions on YouTube and the GDN.

Reach: Target users based on demographics, interests, or specific YouTube channels/videos.

Ad Format: In-stream ads (played before, during, or after a video), video discovery ads (displayed in search results or related video recommendations), or bumper ads (short non-skippable ads).

IV. Shopping Campaigns:

- Goal: Promote and sell products directly from your e-commerce website by displaying product listings (including images, prices, and descriptions) in search results.
- Reach: Target users searching for specific products on Google.
- Ad Format: Product listing ads showcasing your inventory.

V. App Campaigns:

- Goal: Promote mobile apps across Google's properties, including Google Search, YouTube, Google Play, and the GDN, to increase app installs or in-app actions.
- Reach: Target users based on their interests, behaviors, or app usage patterns.

- Ad Format: Text, image, video, or HTML5 ads promoting the app.

VI. Discovery Campaigns:

- Goal: Showcase your products, services, or content to potential customers as they browse Google Discover, YouTube home feed, and Gmail promotions tab.
- Reach: Leverage Google's machine learning algorithms to reach users interested in relevant content.
- Ad Format: Image or carousel ads with headlines, descriptions, and images.

Each campaign type offers different targeting options, bidding strategies, and ad formats to optimize your ad performance. Choosing the right campaign type and goal depends on your marketing objectives and target audience. It's important to monitor and optimize your campaigns regularly to maximize your return on investment (ROI) and achieve your desired outcomes.

B. Campaign settings and options

Google Ads offers a variety of campaign settings and options that allow advertisers to customize their advertising campaigns to reach their target audience effectively. These settings and options play a crucial role in determining how and where ads are displayed, as well as how much advertisers are willing to pay for each click or conversion.

Let's explore the key campaign settings and options in Google Ads:

➢ Campaign Type: Google Ads provides different campaign types to suit specific advertising goals. The available options include Search Network campaigns (text ads on search engine results pages), Display Network campaigns (banner and text ads on websites), Video campaigns (ads on YouTube and other video platforms), Shopping campaigns (product listing ads), and App campaigns (promoting mobile apps).

➢ Campaign Subtype: Within each campaign type, advertisers can choose subtypes that further define the campaign's focus. For instance, within Search Network campaigns, advertisers can opt for standard campaigns, dynamic search ads, or call-only campaigns. Similarly, Shopping campaigns have subtypes like standard Shopping or Smart Shopping campaigns.

➢ Campaign Name and Budget: Advertisers should provide a meaningful name for their campaign to easily identify it in the account. Setting a daily or monthly budget ensures control over ad spend, allowing advertisers to specify the maximum amount they are willing to spend on their campaign within a specific timeframe.

➢ Network Settings: Advertisers can choose where their ads will appear by selecting the network settings. Google Ads offers two primary options: Search Network and Display Network. The Search Network displays ads on search engine results pages, while the Display Network showcases ads on websites, mobile apps, and YouTube.

➢ Locations and Languages: Advertisers can target specific geographic locations where they want their ads to appear. This can be as broad as targeting an entire country or as specific as targeting a particular city or region. Language targeting helps advertisers reach users who speak a particular language.

➢ Bidding and Budget Settings: Google Ads provides various bidding strategies, including manual CPC (Cost-Per-Click), enhanced CPC, target CPA (Cost-Per-Acquisition), and target ROAS (Return on Ad Spend). Advertisers can choose the strategy that aligns with their goals and set bids accordingly.

Additionally, budget settings enable advertisers to control their spending at the campaign level.

➢ Ad Extensions: Ad extensions allow advertisers to include additional information or links in their ads, making them more prominent and engaging. Examples of ad extensions include sitelink extensions (additional links to specific pages on the website), call extensions (phone number displayed with the ad), and location extensions (business address shown with the ad).

➢ Ad Schedule: With ad scheduling, advertisers can choose specific days and times when their ads should be displayed. This feature is particularly useful for businesses targeting specific hours of the day or days of the week when their target audience is most active or likely to convert.

➢ Ad Rotation: Ad rotation settings determine how often different ads in an ad group are displayed. Advertisers can choose between "optimize for clicks" to show the ads that are expected to get the most clicks or "rotate indefinitely" to evenly distribute ad impressions.

➢ Conversion Tracking: Conversion tracking allows advertisers to measure the effectiveness of their campaigns by tracking specific actions users take on their websites, such as purchases, form submissions, or sign-ups. By setting up conversion tracking, advertisers can optimize their campaigns based on actual performance data.

These are some of the essential campaign settings and options available in Google Ads. Advertisers should carefully consider and customize these settings based on their advertising goals, target audience, and budget to maximize the effectiveness of their campaigns and achieve desired results.

C. Creating ad groups

Creating ad groups is an essential step in setting up an effective Google Ads campaign. Ad groups allow you to organize your ads and keywords into targeted themes, enabling you to deliver relevant ads to specific audiences and improve your campaign's overall performance. Let's dive into the process of creating ad groups and some best practices to follow:

➢ Campaign Structure: Before creating ad groups, ensure that you have a well-structured campaign in place. A campaign represents your overall advertising objective, and ad groups are the building blocks within it. Determine the specific goals, target audience, and budget for your campaign.

➤ Identify Themes: Each ad group should revolve around a specific theme or product category. For example, if you're running a campaign for an online shoe store, you might create ad groups for different shoe types like sneakers, sandals, or boots. This helps in tailoring your ad messaging and targeting for better performance.

➤ Keyword Research: Conduct thorough keyword research to identify relevant keywords for each ad group. Use tools like Google Keyword Planner or third-party tools to find keywords with appropriate search volumes and relevance to your ad group's theme. Aim for a mix of broad, phrase, and exact match keywords to cover different search intents.

➤ Ad Copy Creation: Craft compelling ad copies that align with the keywords and theme of each ad group. Your ads should highlight the unique selling points of your products or services and include a strong call-to-action. Tailor your ad copy to match the language and tone preferred by your target audience.

➤ Landing Pages: Ensure that each ad group directs users to a dedicated and relevant landing page on your website. The landing page should provide a seamless experience by delivering the information or offer promised in the ad. Optimizing landing pages for conversion and usability can positively impact your ad group's performance.

➤ Ad Group Settings: Set up specific targeting options and settings for each ad group. You can define location targeting, language preferences, ad scheduling, and device preferences based on the characteristics of your target audience. Utilize audience targeting options, such as demographics, interests, or remarketing, if applicable.

➤ Ad Group Optimization: Continuously monitor and optimize your ad groups to improve their performance. Analyze key metrics like click-through rate (CTR), conversion rate, and cost per conversion. Make data-driven decisions to adjust bids, pause underperforming keywords, test new ad variations, or refine targeting settings.

➤ Ad Group Expansion: As your campaign progresses, consider expanding your ad groups to cover additional relevant themes or keywords. Regularly evaluate your search term reports to discover new keywords or negative keywords to include or exclude from your ad groups. This helps to refine and grow your campaign over time.

Remember, creating well-organized ad groups with targeted keywords and compelling ad copies can enhance the effectiveness of your Google Ads campaign. Regularly monitor, test, and optimize your ad groups to achieve optimal results.

D. Writing compelling Ad copy

Writing compelling ad copy is crucial for the success of your Google Ads campaigns. It is the text that appears in your ads and plays a significant role in attracting users' attention, conveying your message, and driving them to take action. Here are some key points to consider when writing compelling ad copy:

➤ Understand your audience: Before crafting your ad copy, it's essential to have a clear understanding of your target audience. Research their demographics, interests, and pain points. This knowledge will help you tailor your ad copy to resonate with their needs and motivations.

➤ Highlight unique selling points: Identify what sets your product or service apart from the competition. Focus on the unique features, benefits, or offers that make your offering compelling. Highlight these selling points in your ad copy to grab attention and differentiate yourself from other advertisers.

➤ Use attention-grabbing headlines: The headline is the first thing users see in your ad. Make it catchy, concise, and relevant. Use strong, action-oriented language to pique users' curiosity and entice them to learn more. Consider incorporating numbers, questions, or calls to action (CTAs) to make the headline more compelling.

➢ Craft engaging descriptions: The description lines provide an opportunity to expand on the headline and provide more information. Use persuasive language to communicate the value proposition of your product or service. Focus on benefits rather than just features. Highlight how your offering can solve users' problems or improve their lives.

➢ Incorporate relevant keywords: Including relevant keywords in your ad copy is crucial for increasing its relevance and improving your ad's visibility. Align your copy with the keywords you are targeting to ensure a strong connection between the search query and your ad. This can help improve your ad's quality score and ad rank.

➢ Use compelling CTAs: A strong call to action encourages users to take the desired action. Clearly state what action you want users to take, such as "Buy Now," "Sign Up Today," or "Learn More." Create a sense of urgency or offer incentives, such as limited-time discounts or free trials, to motivate users to act immediately.

➢ Test and iterate: Writing compelling ad copy is an iterative process. Create multiple variations of your ads and test them to identify what works best. Experiment with different headlines, descriptions, CTAs, and messaging strategies. Use A/B testing to compare the performance of different ad variations and refine your copy based on data-driven insights.

➢ Maintain relevance with landing pages: Ensure a strong alignment between your ad copy and the landing page users are directed to. The landing page should deliver on the promises made in your ad and provide a seamless user experience. Consistency between ad copy and landing page increases trust and improves conversion rates.

➢ Monitor and optimize: Regularly monitor the performance of your ads and make data-driven optimizations. Analyze metrics like click-through rate (CTR), conversion rate, and cost per conversion to evaluate the effectiveness of your ad copy. Continuously refine your copy based on insights gained from the performance data.

Remember, compelling ad copy should be concise, relevant, and persuasive. By understanding your audience, highlighting unique selling points, using attention-grabbing headlines, crafting engaging descriptions, incorporating relevant keywords, using compelling CTAs, testing and iterating, maintaining relevance with landing pages, and monitoring and optimizing your ads, you can create compelling ad copy that drives better results in your Google Ads campaigns.

E. Ad extensions and their benefits

Ad extensions are additional pieces of information or interactive elements that can be added to your Google Ads campaigns. They enhance your ads by providing extra details, additional links, or interactive features, making them more informative and engaging for potential customers. Ad extensions serve as valuable tools to maximize your ad's visibility and improve the overall performance of your advertising campaigns.

Here are some commonly used ad extensions and their benefits:

1. Sitelink Extensions: Sitelinks allow you to add additional links to specific pages on your website, giving users more options to navigate directly to relevant sections. They help users find what they are looking for quickly, increasing the chances of conversions. Sitelinks also occupy more space on the search results page, making your ad more prominent and improving click-through rates.

2. Call Extensions: Call extensions enable users to call your business directly from the ad by displaying your phone number. This extension is particularly effective for businesses that rely on phone calls, such as local service providers or restaurants. By making it convenient for users to contact you, call extensions can drive more phone leads and conversions.

3. Location Extensions: Location extensions display your business address alongside your ad, making it easier for potential customers to find your physical store. This is especially valuable for brick-and-mortar businesses as it increases foot traffic and improves local visibility. Users can click on the address to get directions, enhancing the chances of in-store visits.

4. Callout Extensions: Callout extensions allow you to highlight specific features or benefits of your products or services within your ad. This extension can be used to emphasize free shipping, 24/7 customer support, price matching, or any unique selling point. By providing additional information, callout extensions help increase the relevance and appeal of your ads.

5. Structured Snippet Extensions: Structured snippets enable you to showcase specific aspects or categories of your products or services. They provide additional context and information about your offerings, helping users understand what you provide before they click on your ad. This extension is beneficial for businesses with diverse product lines or services.

6. Price Extensions: Price extensions display a list of your products or services along with their respective prices. Users can view different options and their costs directly in the ad, reducing friction in the decision-making process.

This extension is particularly effective for e-commerce businesses and helps improve the click-through rate and conversion rate.

The benefits of using ad extensions include:

1. Improved Ad Performance: Ad extensions enhance the visibility and attractiveness of your ads, leading to higher click-through rates, increased ad relevance, and improved Quality Scores. This, in turn, can lead to better ad positions, lower costs per click, and ultimately, improved return on investment (ROI).

2. Enhanced User Experience: Ad extensions provide users with more information and options, making it easier for them to find what they need and take action. By offering additional links, phone numbers, addresses, or snippets of information, you enhance the overall user experience, increasing the likelihood of engagement and conversions.

3. Increased Ad Space: Ad extensions expand the size of your ads, occupying more real estate on the search results page. This not only makes your ads more prominent but also pushes down competing ads, increasing your visibility and driving more traffic to your website.

4. Higher Relevance: By including relevant information through ad extensions, you can improve the overall relevance of your ads. This leads to more qualified clicks and higher conversion rates as users are more likely to engage with ads that align with their specific needs and interests.

5. Cost-Efficiency: Ad extensions are free to add to your campaigns. While you pay for clicks, interactions, or conversions, there is no additional cost associated with implementing ad extensions. This means you can enhance your ads' performance and user experience without increasing your advertising budget.

CHAPTER FIVE: UNDERSTANDING QUALITY SCORE AND AD RANK

A. What is Quality Score?

Quality Score is a metric used in Google Ads that measures the relevance and quality of your keywords, ads, and landing pages. It plays a crucial role in determining the position of your ads and the cost per click (CPC) you pay.

In simple terms, Quality Score reflects how well your ad campaign aligns with the user's search query and the overall user experience. It ranges from 1 to 10, with 10 being the highest score. The higher your Quality Score, the better your ad's performance and the lower your CPC.

Several factors contribute to calculating Quality Score:

➤ Click-through rate (CTR): Google considers the historical CTR of your keyword and ad in relation to its position on the search results page. A higher CTR indicates greater relevance and quality, resulting in a higher Quality Score.

➤ Ad relevance: The relevance of your ad to the user's search query is crucial. Google examines how closely your keyword matches the ad text and the search intent. Relevant ads tend to have higher Quality Scores.

➢ Landing page experience: Google evaluates the quality and relevance of the landing page that users are directed to when they click on your ad. A well-designed, user-friendly, and informative landing page that matches the intent of the ad can positively impact your Quality Score.

➢ Historical performance: The historical performance of your Google Ads account is considered. This includes the overall CTR of your ads, the quality of your landing pages, and the relevance of your keywords over time.

A higher Quality Score brings several benefits:

1. Improved ad position: Higher Quality Scores can lead to higher ad rankings, increasing the visibility of your ads on the search results page.

2. Lower CPC: With a higher Quality Score, you can secure better ad positions while paying less for each click. This can result in significant cost savings and better return on investment (ROI) for your ad campaign.

3. Ad extensions eligibility: Quality Score also affects the eligibility of your ads for ad extensions, such as sitelink extensions, call extensions, and structured snippets. Higher Quality Scores improve the chances of your ads being

displayed with these additional features, enhancing your ad's visibility and performance.

To improve your Quality Score, focus on the following actions:

1. Keyword optimization: Conduct thorough keyword research and select relevant keywords that closely match the intent of your target audience. Group them into tightly themed ad groups to improve relevance.

2. Compelling ad copy: Craft persuasive ad copy that incorporates your keywords and resonates with the user's search query. Make sure the ad is clear, concise, and compelling.

3. Landing page optimization: Enhance your landing pages to provide a seamless user experience. Ensure that the landing page content is relevant to the ad and offers valuable information or solutions to the user.

4. Regular campaign monitoring and optimization: Continuously monitor the performance of your campaigns, identifying and eliminating underperforming keywords and ads. Test different variations to find what works best and make data-driven decisions to optimize your campaigns.

Remember, Quality Score is a dynamic metric that can change over time based on the performance of your ads and landing pages. By consistently focusing on improving relevance, user experience, and performance, you can increase your Quality Score and achieve better results with your Google Ads campaigns.

B. Factors influencing Quality Score

Quality Score is a crucial metric in Google Ads that determines the effectiveness and cost of your ad campaigns. It's a rating ranging from 1 to 10 that Google assigns to each keyword in your account, representing the quality and relevance of your ads and landing pages. A higher Quality Score can lead to better ad positions, lower costs, and improved overall campaign performance. Several factors influence Quality Score, and understanding them is essential for optimizing your campaigns. Here are the key factors:

➢ Click-Through Rate (CTR): CTR is the ratio of users who click on your ad to the number of impressions it receives. It is one of the most significant factors in Quality Score. Higher CTR indicates that your ads are relevant and appealing to users, leading to better Quality Scores.

➢ Ad Relevance: The relevance of your ad to the search query is crucial. Google assesses how well your ad matches the intent of the user's search. Creating highly targeted and specific ad groups with relevant keywords helps improve ad relevance.

➢ Landing Page Experience: Google considers the quality and relevancy of the landing page users are directed to when they click on your ad. A well-designed landing page that offers valuable content and a seamless user experience can positively impact Quality Score.

➢ Ad Format and Extensions: The format and extensions you use in your ads also play a role in Quality Score. Utilizing ad extensions, such as sitelinks, callouts, and structured snippets, enhances your ad's visibility and relevancy, potentially leading to higher Quality Score

➢ Historical Account Performance: Google takes into account the historical performance of your Google Ads account. This includes factors like overall CTR, ad relevance, and landing page experience. Consistently maintaining good performance can positively impact your Quality Score.

➢ Keyword Performance: The performance of keywords within your ad groups affects Quality Score. If certain keywords have low CTR or poor relevance, it can bring down the overall Quality Score. Regularly reviewing and optimizing your keyword list is crucial for improving performance.

➤ Ad Performance on Display Network: If you are running display campaigns, the performance of your ads on the Google Display Network can impact Quality Score. Relevance, CTR, and landing page experience on display placements should be monitored and optimized.

➤ Geographic Performance: Quality Score can vary based on the geographic location where your ads are being shown. Factors such as user behavior, competition, and ad performance in specific locations can influence Quality Score.

It's important to note that Quality Score is dynamic and can change over time based on the performance of your ads and landing pages. Regularly monitoring your campaigns, optimizing ad copy, refining keywords, and improving landing page experience are essential to maintain and improve your Quality Scores.

C. Improving Quality Score

Improving Quality Score is a crucial aspect of optimizing Google Ads campaigns. Quality Score is a metric used by Google to determine the relevance and quality of your keywords, ads, and landing pages. It plays a significant role in determining your ad rankings and the cost per click (CPC) you pay.

To improve your Quality Score, consider the following strategies:

➢ Keyword Relevance: Ensure that your keywords are highly relevant to your ad groups and landing pages. Create tightly themed ad groups with closely related keywords to enhance the relevance between your keywords and ads.

➢ Ad Relevance: Craft compelling and targeted ads that closely match the intent of the searcher. Include the keyword in your ad copy to reinforce relevance. Use ad extensions such as sitelinks, callouts, and structured snippets to provide additional information and make your ads more appealing.

➢ Landing Page Experience: Create landing pages that are relevant to the keywords and ads. Make sure the landing pages load quickly, have clear navigation, and provide valuable content that aligns with the user's search intent. Ensure a mobile-friendly experience and optimize your landing pages for conversions.

➢ Click-Through Rate (CTR): A high CTR indicates that your ads are attracting user attention and are relevant. To boost CTR, write compelling ad copy, use relevant ad extensions, and test different variations of your ads to identify what resonates best with your audience.

➢ Historical Performance: The historical performance of your account, including CTR and Quality Score, can impact your current Quality Score. Continuously optimize your campaigns, ad groups, and keywords to maintain a positive performance history.

➢ Account Structure: Organize your campaigns and ad groups in a logical structure that reflects the hierarchy of your website. This helps improve relevancy and makes it easier to manage and optimize your ads.

➢ Negative Keywords: Regularly review your search terms report and add negative keywords to prevent your ads from appearing for irrelevant searches. This helps improve the overall relevance of your campaigns and boosts your Quality Score.

➢ Ad Testing: Test different variations of your ads to identify what performs best. Experiment with different headlines, descriptions, calls-to-action, and display URLs. Continuously monitor and optimize your ads based on performance data.

➢ Quality Landing Page Experience: Enhance your landing page experience by providing valuable and relevant content, ensuring easy navigation, optimizing page load speed, and making it mobile-friendly. A positive landing page experience can improve your Quality Score.

➤ Relevant Extensions: Utilize ad extensions such as call extensions, site link extensions, and structured snippets to provide additional information and improve the visibility and relevance of your ads.

Remember, improving Quality Score is an ongoing process. Regularly monitor and optimize your campaigns, test different strategies, and make data-driven decisions to improve the overall performance of your Google Ads campaigns.

D. Ad Rank and its importance

Ad Rank is a crucial concept in Google Ads that determines the position and visibility of your ads in search results. It plays a significant role in the success of your ad campaigns and achieving your advertising goals. Ad Rank is calculated using multiple factors, including bid amount, ad quality, and expected impact of ad extensions and formats. Let's delve into these aspects and understand the importance of Ad Rank in more detail.

➤ **Bid Amount:**

The bid amount is the maximum amount you're willing to pay for a click on your ad. Higher bids increase your chances of securing a better position in search results. However, bidding alone does not guarantee a top position. Ad Rank considers other factors as well.

> ➤ **Ad Quality:**

Ad quality is assessed based on various factors, such as the relevance of your ad to the search query, the historical performance of your ad and account, and the quality of your landing page. Google wants to ensure that users see ads that are relevant and useful to them, so ads that offer a better user experience are rewarded with higher ad quality scores.

> ➤ **Expected Impact of Ad Extensions and Formats:**

Ad extensions provide additional information and functionality to your ads, such as call buttons, sitelink extensions, or location information. The expected impact of these extensions on the overall ad performance is taken into account when calculating Ad Rank. The more relevant and valuable your ad extensions are, the higher your Ad Rank can be.

The Importance of Ad Rank:

1. Ad Position:
   Ad Rank determines the position of your ad in search results. A higher Ad Rank increases the likelihood of your ad appearing in a top position, leading to greater visibility and exposure. Being among the top positions can significantly increase the chances of attracting clicks and driving relevant traffic to your website.

2. Cost-Effectiveness:
   Ad Rank helps to optimize the cost-effectiveness of your campaigns. By considering factors beyond bid amount, Google aims to show ads that provide the best user experience. This means that even if your bid is lower than competitors, a higher ad quality can still result in a better position, allowing you to achieve your advertising goals more efficiently.

3. Ad Extensions and Formats:
   Ad Rank considers the expected impact of ad extensions and formats. By using relevant and valuable extensions, you can enhance your Ad Rank and provide more useful information to users. This can result in higher click-through rates, increased engagement, and improved campaign performance.

4. Ad Auction Insights:
   Ad Rank is crucial for understanding your competitive landscape. Ad Auction Insights provides information about how your ads are performing in comparison to other advertisers. By monitoring your Ad Rank and comparing it to your competitors, you can gain insights into areas where improvements are needed and identify opportunities to outperform them.

By considering factors like bid amount, ad quality, and expected impact of ad extensions and formats, it helps you achieve optimal ad positions, improve cost-effectiveness, increase click-through rates, and gain a competitive edge in the advertising landscape.

CHAPTER SIX: BIDDING STRATEGIES AND BUDGETING

A. Different bidding strategies

There are various bidding strategies available in Google Ads that advertisers can use to optimize their campaigns and achieve their marketing goals. Each bidding strategy has its own benefits and considerations. Here are some of the different bidding strategies you can employ:

> Manual CPC (Cost-Per-Click): With manual CPC, you manually set the maximum amount you're willing to pay for each click on your ads. It provides full control over your bids, allowing you to adjust bids based on performance and target specific keywords or placements.

> Target CPA (Cost-Per-Acquisition): Target CPA bidding uses machine learning to automatically set bids to achieve a specific cost-per-acquisition goal. You need to set a target CPA, and the system optimizes your bids to drive conversions at or near that cost.

> Target ROAS (Return on Ad Spend): Target ROAS bidding is focused on maximizing the return on your advertising spend. You set a target ROAS, and the system automatically adjusts your bids to maximize revenue within that goal. This strategy is suitable for

businesses with a defined return on investment (ROI) goal.

➤ Enhanced CPC: Enhanced CPC is a bidding strategy that adjusts your manual bids in real-time based on the likelihood of conversion. Google Ads uses historical conversion data and various signals to increase or decrease your bids for specific clicks. It helps maximize conversions while still allowing some manual control.

➤ Maximize Clicks: This strategy is designed to drive as many clicks as possible within your budget. The system automatically sets bids to get the most clicks, without considering conversion rates. It is suitable for campaigns focused on generating website traffic or increasing brand visibility.

➤ Maximize Conversions: With this strategy, the system automatically sets bids to get the maximum number of conversions within your budget. It uses historical data and machine learning to optimize bids based on conversion likelihood.

➤ Maximize Conversion Value: This bidding strategy aims to maximize the total conversion value within your budget. It adjusts bids to focus on higher-value conversions, such as sales with larger order sizes or higher average transaction values.

➢ Target Impression Share: This strategy allows you to specify the desired impression share you want your ads to have in the auction. Impression share represents the percentage of times your ads are shown compared to the total number of eligible impressions. This strategy helps increase brand visibility and market share.

➢ Cost-Per-Thousand Impressions (CPM): CPM bidding is suitable for campaigns focused on increasing brand awareness. Instead of paying for clicks or conversions, you pay for every thousand impressions your ad receives. It can be useful for display or video campaigns.

It's important to choose a bidding strategy that aligns with your campaign goals, budget, and level of control you want. It's recommended to test and monitor the performance of different bidding strategies to find the most effective approach for your specific advertising objectives.

B. Setting up bid adjustments

Bid adjustments in Google Ads allow you to modify your keyword bids based on various targeting factors such as device, location, time of day, and audience. These adjustments help you optimize your ad campaign and reach your target audience more effectively. Let's explore how to set up bid adjustments in Google Ads.

1. Sign in to your Google Ads account and navigate to the campaign or ad group where you want to set up bid adjustments.

2. Click on the "Settings" tab and select "Devices," "Locations," "Ad schedule," or "Audiences" based on the factor you want to adjust bids for.

3. Device Bid Adjustments:
   - Click on the "Devices" tab and you'll see a list of devices such as computers, mobile devices, and tablets.
   - Enter a bid adjustment percentage for each device. For example, if you want to increase bids for mobile devices by 10%, enter "+10%". If you want to decrease bids for tablets by 20%, enter "-20%". You can also set a -100% adjustment to exclude a particular device.
   - Click "Save" to apply the device bid adjustments.

4. Location Bid Adjustments:
   - Click on the "Locations" tab and you can either add new locations or modify bids for existing ones.

   - To add new locations, click on the "Edit" button and select "Add Locations". You can enter specific locations, target by radius around a location, or choose entire regions or countries.

   - To modify bids for existing locations, click on the "Bid adj." column and enter the bid adjustment percentage. Similar to device adjustments, use + or - symbols to increase or decrease bids.

   - Click "Save" to apply the location bid adjustments.

5. Ad Schedule Bid Adjustments:
   - Click on the "Ad schedule" tab and you'll see a grid representing days and times.

   - To adjust bids for specific times, click on the "Bid adj." column for the desired time slot and enter the adjustment percentage.

   - You can increase or decrease bids for specific days and times based on performance trends or customer behavior.
   - Click "Save" to apply the ad schedule bid adjustments.

6. Audience Bid Adjustments:
   - Click on the "Audiences" tab and you can target or exclude specific audiences.

   - To add audiences, click on the "Edit" button and select "Add audiences". You can choose from various audience categories such as demographics, interests, or remarketing lists.

   - To modify bids for existing audiences, click on the "Bid adj." column and enter the adjustment percentage.

   - You can increase bids to reach more valuable audiences or decrease bids for less relevant ones.

   - Click "Save" to apply the audience bid adjustments.

It's important to monitor the performance of your bid adjustments regularly and make necessary optimizations based on the data. Experiment with different bid adjustments to find the right balance that maximizes your campaign's performance.

Remember, bid adjustments should be used strategically to align with your campaign goals and target audience preferences.

C. Budgeting and campaign spending

Budgeting and campaign spending are crucial aspects of running successful Google Ads campaigns. Effective budget management ensures that your advertising budget is allocated efficiently and maximizes the return on investment (ROI) for your advertising efforts. Let's dive into the key considerations and strategies for budgeting and campaign spending in Google Ads.

> Set a Realistic Budget: Start by determining the overall budget you are willing to allocate to Google Ads. Consider your business goals, target audience, and the competitiveness of your industry. A realistic budget should be based on your advertising objectives, revenue targets, and the cost-per-click (CPC) of your keywords.

> Determine Campaign Objectives: Clearly define the objectives for each campaign, whether it's to increase website traffic, generate leads, boost sales, or raise brand awareness. Having specific goals will help you allocate your budget more effectively.

> Keyword Research: Thoroughly research keywords related to your business to identify their search volume and average CPC. This research will help you estimate the budget needed to achieve your desired results. Use the Google Keyword Planner or other keyword research tools to gain insights into keyword performance.

➤ Bid Strategy: Select an appropriate bidding strategy based on your goals. Google Ads offers various bidding options, such as manual CPC, enhanced CPC, target CPA, and target ROAS. Each strategy has its advantages and should align with your budget and objectives. For example, if your primary goal is to increase conversions, you may opt for a target CPA strategy.

➤ Ad Scheduling: Analyze your campaign performance data to identify the most effective days and times for running your ads. Adjust your campaign settings to allocate more budget during peak hours or days when your target audience is most active.

➤ Campaign Performance Monitoring: Continuously monitor the performance of your campaigns to identify opportunities for optimization. Track key metrics like click-through rate (CTR), conversion rate, cost per conversion, and ROI. Allocate more budget to high-performing campaigns and keywords while reducing or pausing underperforming ones.

➤ Testing and Optimization: Allocate a portion of your budget for testing new ad creatives, landing pages, and targeting options. Conduct A/B tests to compare different variations and identify the most effective elements. Continuously optimize your campaigns based on data-driven insights to improve performance and maximize your budget's impact.

➢ Ad Extensions and Quality Score: Utilize ad extensions like site links, callouts, and structured snippets to enhance your ad's visibility and engagement. Additionally, focus on improving your Quality Score by optimizing ad relevance, landing page experience, and expected click-through rate. A higher Quality Score can lead to better ad positions and lower CPCs.

➢ Remarketing and Audience Targeting: Leverage remarketing to reach users who have previously visited your website or engaged with your brand. Allocate a portion of your budget to targeting these warm leads, as they are more likely to convert. Experiment with audience targeting options such as demographics, interests, and custom intent to narrow down your target audience and maximize your budget's efficiency.

➢ Regular Budget Reviews: Review your campaign performance and budget allocation regularly. Adjust your budget based on your campaign's performance, market conditions, and business objectives. Take advantage of Google Ads' reporting features to gain insights into your spending patterns and make informed decisions.

Remember, effective budgeting and campaign spending require ongoing monitoring, optimization, and adaptation. Continuously analyze your data, test new strategies, and refine your campaigns to achieve optimal results within your allocated budget.

CHAPTER SEVEN: AD FORMATS AND DISPLAY ADVERTISING

A. Different ad formats in Google Ads

There are several ad formats available in Google Ads that cater to different advertising goals and platforms. Each format has its own unique features and specifications.

Here, I'll provide a concise explanation of the main ad formats in Google Ads:

1. Text Ads: These are the simplest and most common ad format in Google Ads. Text ads consist of a headline, two lines of description, and a display URL. They appear on the search engine results page and partner websites.

2. Image Ads: These ads incorporate visual elements to attract attention. Image ads can be static or animated, and they are displayed on the Google Display Network (GDN). Advertisers can create image ads in various sizes and formats.

3. Responsive Ads: These ads automatically adjust their size, appearance, and format to fit available ad spaces. Advertisers provide headlines, descriptions, images, and logos, and Google Ads optimizes the ad combinations to achieve the best performance on the GDN.

4. App Promotion Ads: Specifically designed for mobile app advertising, these ads encourage users to download or engage with an app. App promotion ad can include text, images, and call-to-action buttons. They appear on the GDN and within other apps.

5. Video Ads: These ads utilize video content to convey messages effectively. Advertisers can create video ads in various formats, such as in-stream ads (played before, during, or after YouTube videos) and out-stream ads (displayed in mobile apps and websites).

6. Showcase Shopping Ads: Primarily for retail advertisers, showcase shopping ads allow you to group related products together. When users search for broad terms, these ads display a collection of products, enabling advertisers to showcase their brand and offerings.

7. Discovery Ads: These visually-rich ads appear in various Google-owned properties, including YouTube, Gmail, and the Discover feed on the Google app. Discovery ads are designed to capture users' attention as they explore content.

8. Call-Only Ads: With call-only ads, advertisers focus on driving phone calls to their business. These ads appear on

mobile devices, and when users click on them, they are directly connected to the advertiser via phone call.

9. App Engagement Ads: These ads are used to re-engage users who have already installed app. App engagement ads promote specific features, encourage in-app actions, or entice users back to the app.

10. Shopping Ads: Designed for e-commerce businesses, shopping ads showcase products with images, prices, and store information. They appear at the top of search results and in the "Shopping" tab. Shopping ads require a product feed and are managed through Google Merchant Center.

It's worth noting that Google Ads regularly introduces new ad formats and updates existing ones, so it's essential to stay updated with the latest offerings.

B. Creating effective display ads

Creating effective display ads is crucial for a successful Google Ads campaign. Display ads are visual advertisements that appear on websites within the Google Display Network (GDN). To maximize their effectiveness, consider the following key aspects:

➢ Clear and Compelling Message: Craft a concise and impactful message that communicates the main benefit or value proposition of your product or service. Use persuasive language and focus on what sets your offering apart from competitors. Be clear and avoid ambiguity to ensure your message resonates with the target audience.

➢ Eye-catching Design: Capture attention with visually appealing and professional designs. Use high-quality images or graphics that align with your brand and create a positive impression. Choose colors, fonts, and layout that are visually pleasing and consistent with your brand's style guidelines.

➢ Strong Call to Action (CTA): Include a clear and prominent CTA to guide users on the desired action, such as "Buy Now," "Learn More," or "Sign Up." Make sure the CTA stands out and is easily clickable. Consider using actionable language and urgency to encourage immediate engagement.

➤ Relevant Targeting: Define your target audience based on demographics, interests, behaviors, or remarketing lists. Align your ad content with the interests and preferences of the intended viewers. By showing relevant ads to the right audience, you increase the chances of engagement and conversions.

➤ Responsive Ad Design: Opt for responsive ad formats that automatically adjust their size and appearance to fit various ad spaces across different devices. This ensures your ads look visually appealing and legible on desktops, laptops, tablets, and mobile devices.

➤ Effective Landing Page: Create a landing page that provides a seamless transition from the ad. The landing page should reinforce the ad's message and offer further information or a conversion opportunity. Ensure the landing page is mobile-friendly, loads quickly, and has a clear path for users to complete the desired action.

➤ A/B Testing: Experiment with different ad variations to identify the most effective elements. Test different headlines, images, CTAs, and ad formats to understand what resonates best with your audience. Continuously monitor and optimize your campaigns based on the insights gained from A/B testing.

➢ Remarketing: Utilize remarketing campaigns to target users who have previously interacted with your website or app. Tailor your display ads to remind them of their interest or showcase complementary products/services. Remarketing helps maintain brand visibility and can lead to higher conversion rates.

➢ Ad Extensions: Take advantage of ad extensions to provide additional information or features alongside your display ads. Extensions such as sitelinks, call buttons, or location information can enhance the visibility and effectiveness of your ads, driving higher engagement and click-through rates.

➢ Performance Tracking and Optimization: Regularly monitor the performance of your display ads using Google Ads' analytics tools. Identify metrics such as click-through rate (CTR), conversion rate, and cost per conversion to assess the effectiveness of your campaigns. Optimize your ads based on data insights, making adjustments to targeting, messaging, or design elements to improve results.

By focusing on these key aspects and continuously refining your display ad strategy, you can create more effective and engaging campaigns that drive desired outcomes for your business.

C. Display network targeting options

Display network targeting options refer to the various methods and strategies available within Google Ads to reach your desired audience on the Google Display Network. The Display Network is a collection of websites, apps, and videos where advertisers can display their ads to potential customers.

1. **Keywords**: You can select specific keywords related to your products or services to target relevant websites and pages. Google analyzes the content of websites and matches them with your selected keywords to determine ad placements.

2. **Topics**: Instead of selecting individual keywords, you can choose broad topics that align with your target audience's interests or the theme of your ad. Google will display your ads on websites and pages that cover those topics.

3. **Placements**: With placement targeting, you have the ability to choose specific websites, apps, or even individual pages where you want your ads to appear. This option allows for precise control over ad placement but may limit your reach compared to other targeting methods.

4. **Audiences**: Google provides various audience targeting options to reach specific groups of people. These include:

a. Affinity Audiences: Reach users who have demonstrated a strong interest in specific topics or industries based on their browsing behavior and online activities.

b. In-Market Audiences: Target users who are actively researching or considering purchasing products or services similar to what you offer.

c. Custom Intent Audiences: Create custom audiences based on specific keywords or URLs related to your target audience's interests or purchase intent.

d. Similar Audiences: Reach users who share similar characteristics with your existing customers or website visitors.

e. Remarketing: Show ads to users who have previously visited your website or engaged with your app. This helps to re-engage potential customers who have shown interest in your offerings.

5. **Demographics**: You can refine your targeting based on specific demographic factors such as age, gender, parental status, or household income. This option allows you to tailor your ads to the characteristics of your ideal customers.

6. **Placement Exclusions**: To avoid displaying ads on certain websites or pages that may not align with your brand or

marketing goals, you can specify exclusions. This helps you maintain brand safety and ensures your ads appear in suitable environments.

It's important to note that you can combine multiple targeting options to create highly targeted campaigns. By carefully selecting and testing different targeting methods, you can maximize the effectiveness of your display network campaigns and reach the right audience with your ads. Regular monitoring and optimization are crucial to ensure your ads are performing well and achieving your desired outcomes.

CHAPTER EIGHT: TRACKING AND MEASURING PERFORMANCE

A. Setting up conversion tracking

Setting up conversion tracking in Google Ads is a crucial step for measuring the effectiveness of your advertising campaigns and optimizing them for better results. Conversion tracking allows you to track specific actions that users take on your website after clicking on your ads, such as making a purchase, filling out a form, or subscribing to a newsletter. By setting up conversion tracking, you gain valuable insights into the performance of your ads and can make data-driven decisions to improve your return on investment (ROI). To set up conversion tracking in Google Ads, follow these steps:

I. Define your conversion actions: Start by identifying the specific actions on your website that you consider valuable, such as completing a purchase or submitting a lead form. These actions will be the basis for your conversion tracking setup.

II. Choose a conversion tracking method: Google Ads provides different methods to track conversions based on your website setup and technical expertise. The most common methods are:

a. Website tracking: This method involves placing a conversion tracking code, known as a "tag" or "pixel," on the webpage that signifies a completed conversion. Google provides a snippet of code that you or your web developer can add to the relevant pages.

b. Google Analytics integration: If you have Google Analytics set up for your website, you can link it to your Google Ads account. This integration allows you to import your Google Analytics goals and transactions into Google Ads as conversions, without requiring additional code placement.

c. Google Tag Manager: If you use Google Tag Manager, it provides a convenient way to manage all your tracking codes in one place. You can create a conversion tracking tag in Google Tag Manager and deploy it on your website without the need for manual code edits.

III. **Create conversion actions in Google Ads**: Once you've chosen your tracking method, navigate to the "Conversions" section in your Google Ads account. Click on the "+ Conversion" button to start creating a new conversion action. Provide relevant details such as the conversion name, value (if applicable), and the type of action (e.g., purchase, form submission).

IV. Set up conversion tracking code or import goals: Depending on the method you selected, follow the appropriate steps:

a. Website tracking: If you chose website tracking, Google Ads will generate a unique snippet of code for each conversion action you create. Copy and paste this code onto the respective webpage or in the confirmation page that appears after the conversion action.

b. Google Analytics integration: If you opted for the Google Analytics integration method, you need to link your Google Ads and Google Analytics accounts. Then, you can import the desired goals or transactions from Google Analytics into your Google Ads account as conversions.

c. Google Tag Manager: If you're using Google Tag Manager, create a new conversion tracking tag and configure it to fire on the desired conversion event. Publish the changes in Google Tag Manager to start tracking conversions.

V. **Test and verify your setup**: After implementing the conversion tracking code or importing goals, it's crucial to test and verify that it's working correctly. Use Google's Tag Assistant or the Google Analytics Real-Time reports to confirm that conversions are being recorded accurately when the desired actions are completed on your website.

VI. **Set conversion values and attribution models**: Assigning values to your conversions helps you understand the monetary impact of your advertising efforts. For example, if a purchase is worth $100 to your business, you can assign that value to the respective conversion action. Additionally, consider configuring attribution models to determine how credit for conversions is assigned to different ad interactions in the customer journey.

VII. **Monitor and analyze conversion data**: Once your conversion tracking is set up, give it some time to accumulate data. Monitor your conversion metrics regularly in Google Ads, such as conversion volume, conversion rate, and cost per conversion. Analyze the performance of your campaigns based on the conversion data you've collected. Look for trends, patterns, and insights that can help you optimize your ads and improve your campaign's ROI. Pay attention to which keywords, ads, and targeting settings are generating the most conversions, and allocate your budget accordingly.

Some additional tips for setting up conversion tracking:

1. Use the appropriate conversion tracking method based on your website's structure and technical capabilities. If you're not sure which method to choose, consult with a web developer or digital marketing expert.

2. Place the conversion tracking code or tag correctly on your website to ensure accurate tracking. Test the code implementation thoroughly to avoid any technical issues.

3. Consider setting up multiple conversion actions if you have different types of valuable actions on your website. This allows you to track and optimize for each specific conversion event.

4. Regularly review and update your conversion actions. As your business evolves, you may introduce new conversion

actions or modify existing ones. Keep your tracking setup up to date to reflect these changes accurately.

5. Leverage Google's additional conversion tracking features, such as cross-device conversions and offline conversions, if they are applicable to your business. These features provide a more comprehensive view of your conversions and help you understand the full customer journey.

6. Integrate conversion tracking with other tools and platforms, such as CRM systems or email marketing software, to gain a holistic view of your marketing efforts and customer behavior.

Overall, setting up conversion tracking in Google Ads is essential for measuring the effectiveness of your campaigns and making informed decisions for optimization. By accurately tracking conversions, assigning values, and analyzing the data, you can maximize the impact of your advertising and drive better results for your business.

B. Analyzing key performance metrics

Analyzing key performance metrics is a crucial aspect of managing and optimizing Google Ads campaigns. It involves evaluating various metrics to gain insights into the effectiveness and efficiency of your advertising efforts. By understanding these metrics, you can make informed decisions to enhance campaign performance and achieve your advertising goals.

Here are some key performance metrics you should analyze:

➢ Impressions: Impressions indicate the number of times your ads were displayed on the search results page or other websites within the Google Display Network. Monitoring impressions can help you gauge the visibility of your ads and their reach among potential customers.

➢ Clicks: Clicks represent the number of times users clicked on your ads. Analyzing click data helps you assess the overall performance of your ads and determine their click-through rate (CTR), which is the ratio of clicks to impressions. A higher CTR generally indicates more engaging and relevant ads.

➢ Conversion: Conversions signify the actions you want users to take after clicking on your ads, such as making a purchase, submitting a form, or signing up for a newsletter.

Tracking conversions allows you to measure the effectiveness of your campaigns in driving desired outcomes and helps calculate important metrics like conversion rate and cost per conversion.

➢ Cost: Cost refers to the amount of money you spend on your advertising campaigns. It's essential to analyze your costs to ensure that your campaigns remain within your budget and provide a positive return on investment (ROI). You can evaluate metrics like cost per click (CPC) and cost per conversion to assess the efficiency of your spending.

➢ Quality Score: Quality Score is a rating given by Google to assess the relevance and quality of your ads, keywords, and landing pages. A higher Quality Score generally leads to better ad positions and lower costs. Analyzing your Quality Score helps identify areas for improvement and optimize your campaigns for better performance.

➢ Ad Position: Ad position indicates where your ads are displayed on the search results page. Higher ad positions typically generate more visibility and clicks. By analyzing ad positions, you can determine if your ads are appearing in optimal locations and adjust bidding strategies or ad copy to improve performance.

➢ Return on Investment (ROI): ROI measures the profitability of your advertising campaigns by comparing the revenue generated to the costs incurred. Analyzing ROI helps you identify which campaigns are driving the highest returns and allocate your budget effectively. It's crucial to track conversions and attribute them accurately to the appropriate campaigns for accurate ROI calculations.

➢ To effectively analyze these key performance metrics, use Google Ads' reporting and analytics tools. Customize reports to focus on the specific metrics that align with your advertising goals. Regularly monitor and compare metrics over time to identify trends, patterns, and areas that require improvement. This data-driven approach empowers you to make data-backed decisions and optimize your campaigns for better results.

Remember that analyzing key performance metrics is an ongoing process. Continuously monitor and refine your campaigns to adapt to changing market dynamics, user behavior, and industry trends. By staying vigilant and leveraging data-driven insights, you can maximize the effectiveness of your Google Ads campaigns and drive successful advertising outcomes.

C. Using Google Analytics with Google Ads

Google Analytics and Google Ads are powerful tools that can be used together to gain deeper insights into your advertising campaigns and website performance. By linking your Google Analytics and Google Ads accounts, you can unlock valuable data and take more informed actions to optimize your advertising efforts. Here's an extensive explanation of how to use Google Analytics with Google Ads:

1. Linking Google Analytics and Google Ads:

- To get started, ensure that you have both a Google Analytics account and a Google Ads account.
- In Google Ads, navigate to the "Tools & Settings" menu and select "Linked accounts" under the "Setup" section.
- Click on "Google Analytics" and follow the instructions to link your Google Analytics account with your Google Ads account.
- Once linked, you can access Google Analytics data directly from your Google Ads account.

2. Importing Google Analytics goals and metrics:

- After linking the accounts, you can import valuable metrics and goals from Google Analytics into Google Ads.
- In Google Ads, go to the "Tools & Settings" menu and select "Measurement" under the "Setup" section.
- Click on "Conversions" and select "Google Analytics" from the left-hand menu.

- Choose the goals and metrics you want to import, such as e-commerce transactions, page views, or engagement metrics.
- Set up conversion tracking by selecting the appropriate goals and metrics and save the changes.

3. Analyzing Google Analytics data in Google Ads:

- Once the accounts are linked, you can access Google Analytics data directly within Google Ads.
- In your Google Ads account, navigate to the "Reports" tab and select "Predefined reports" or "Custom reports."
- Choose the relevant metrics, dimensions, and segments to analyze the performance of your advertising campaigns.
- Combine Google Analytics data with Google Ads metrics to gain deeper insights into user behavior, conversion paths, and the impact of your advertising efforts.

4. Using Google Analytics audiences in Google Ads:

- Another powerful integration is the ability to use Google Analytics audiences in Google Ads for targeting and remarketing purposes.
- In Google Ads, go to the "Tools & Settings" menu and select "Audience Manager" under the "Shared Library" section.
- Click on "Audiences" and select "Google Analytics" from the left-hand menu.

- Choose the desired audience based on Google Analytics data, such as users who completed specific goals, engaged with particular content, or abandoned a shopping cart.
- Once created, you can use these audiences for targeting or remarketing in your Google Ads campaigns.

5. Optimizing campaigns with Google Analytics insights:

- The integration allows you to leverage Google Analytics data to optimize your Google Ads campaigns effectively.
- Analyze user behavior, bounce rates, time on site, and other metrics to identify areas of improvement on your website.
- Utilize Google Analytics data to optimize your keyword targeting, ad messaging, landing pages, and bidding strategies.
- Use attribution models and assisted conversion data to understand the full customer journey and allocate budgets effectively across different marketing channels.

By using Google Analytics with Google Ads, you can make data-driven decisions and optimize your advertising campaigns based on deeper insights into user behavior, website performance, and the effectiveness of your marketing efforts. The integration provides a comprehensive view of your marketing funnel and empowers you to refine your strategies for better results.

D. A/B testing and optimization techniques

A/B testing and optimization techniques are crucial components of effective Google Ads campaigns. They allow advertisers to experiment with different variations of their ads, landing pages, and targeting settings to identify the most successful combinations that drive the desired outcomes, such as clicks, conversions, or sales. Let's delve into the details of A/B testing and optimization techniques to enhance your understanding.

A/B testing, also known as split testing, involves creating two or more versions of an ad or landing page and comparing their performance to determine which version performs better. This testing methodology helps advertisers make data-driven decisions by evaluating the impact of specific changes on key performance indicators (KPIs).

To conduct an A/B test, you first need to define the element you want to test, such as the ad headline, call-to-action (CTA) button, or landing page layout. Next, create multiple variations of that element, ensuring that only one aspect is altered at a time. For instance, if you're testing ad headlines, keep the ad copy, visuals, and other elements consistent across all versions except for the headlines.

Once your variations are ready, you can set up the A/B test within the Google Ads platform. Specify the percentage of your audience that will see each variation, ensuring that the test is statistically significant. It's essential to provide sufficient time for the test to gather meaningful data, depending on your campaign's traffic volume.

During the test, closely monitor the performance metrics of each variation. Google Ads provides statistical significance indicators to help you determine when a test has reached a reliable conclusion. It's crucial to consider the specific KPIs

you're tracking, such as click-through rate (CTR), conversion rate, cost per conversion, or return on ad spend (ROAS). By comparing the performance of the variations, you can identify the version that outperforms others and generates the desired results.

Optimization techniques come into play once you've identified a winning variation or combination. These techniques involve refining your campaigns to maximize performance and drive better results. Here are some optimization strategies you can implement:

1. Ad Copy Optimization: Continuously test and refine your ad copy by experimenting with different messaging, value propositions, and CTAs. Focus on creating compelling, relevant, and engaging ad content that resonates with your target audience.

2. Keyword Optimization: Regularly review and update your keyword list to ensure it remains relevant and aligned with your campaign goals. Eliminate underperforming keywords and invest more in high-converting ones.

3. Bid Optimization: Adjust your bids based on performance data to optimize your ad placement. Increase bids for top-performing keywords and decrease bids for low-performing ones. You can also leverage automated bidding strategies provided by Google Ads, such as target CPA or target ROAS, to optimize your bids automatically.

4. Ad Extensions: Utilize ad extensions, such as sitelink extensions, call extensions, or location extensions, to enhance the visibility and relevancy of your ads. Test different combinations and placements of ad extensions to improve click-through rates and user engagement.

5. Landing Page Optimization: Optimize your landing pages to improve conversion rates. Test different layouts, headlines, images, forms, and calls-to-action to identify the elements that resonate best with your audience. Ensure a seamless user experience and align your landing page content with the messaging in your ads.

6. Audience Targeting Optimization: Refine your audience targeting by leveraging Google Ads' audience insights and data. Experiment with different targeting options, such as demographics, interests, or remarketing lists, to reach the most relevant audience segments for your campaign.

7. Device and Location Optimization: Analyze performance data by device and location to identify trends and patterns. Adjust bids, messaging, or targeting settings to optimize your campaigns for specific devices or locations that yield better results.

Remember, A/B testing and optimization are ongoing processes. Once you implement changes based on the test results, continue monitoring the performance and iterate further to achieve continuous improvement.

Here are some additional tips to enhance your A/B testing and optimization efforts:

8. Testing Multiple Elements: While A/B testing typically focuses on testing one element at a time, you can also conduct multivariate tests to analyze the impact of multiple elements simultaneously. This allows you to understand how different combinations of elements influence performance.

9. Test at Scale: If you have sufficient data volume, consider running tests across multiple campaigns or ad groups simultaneously. This approach allows you to gather insights more quickly and make broader optimizations across your entire account.

10. Seasonal Variations: Take into account seasonal trends and fluctuations when analyzing test results. Certain changes that may not perform well during specific seasons or events might prove effective at other times. Adjust your optimization strategies accordingly to capitalize on seasonal opportunities.

11. Statistical Significance: Ensure that you gather enough data for your A/B tests to yield statistically significant results. Rely on statistical tools or calculators to determine when you have sufficient data to draw reliable conclusions.

12. Learning from Failures: Not all A/B tests will result in positive outcomes. Embrace failures as learning opportunities. Analyze the data, identify the reasons behind poor performance, and use those insights to iterate and improve future tests.

13. Test Across Channels: Extend your A/B testing and optimization efforts beyond Google Ads. Explore other advertising channels, such as social media platforms or display networks, to test different variations and discover new opportunities for your campaigns.

14. Automation and Machine Learning: Leverage the automation and machine learning capabilities within Google Ads to streamline your A/B testing and optimization processes. Automated bidding, ad rotation, and responsive search ads are examples of features that can help optimize your campaigns based on real-time data.

15. Documentation and Collaboration: Keep detailed records of your A/B testing and optimization experiments, including the variations tested, results, and insights gained. Share this information with your team to foster collaboration, knowledge sharing, and continuous improvement across your organization.

A/B testing and optimization techniques empower advertisers to make data-backed decisions and continually refine their Google Ads campaigns. By testing different elements, measuring performance, and implementing strategic optimizations, you can enhance ad relevance, drive higher engagement, and achieve better campaign outcomes.

CHAPTER NINE: REMARKETING AND AUDIENCE TARGETING

A. Understanding Remarketing

Remarketing is a powerful strategy in Google Ads that allows advertisers to reach out to users who have already interacted with their website or mobile app. It enables businesses to display targeted ads to these previous visitors as they browse other websites or use apps within the Google Display Network or search for relevant keywords on Google.

The key concept behind remarketing is to show tailored ads to users who have already shown some level of interest in your products or services. By doing so, you can reinforce your brand message, increase brand recall, and encourage users to return and complete a desired action, such as making a purchase, filling out a form, or signing up for a newsletter.

Here's how remarketing works in Google Ads:

➢ Setting up Remarketing Lists: To start, you need to create remarketing lists in your Google Ads account. These lists consist of specific groups of users who have performed certain actions on your website or app. For example, you can create a list for users who have added items to their shopping cart but haven't made a purchase.

➢ Adding the Remarketing Tag: Once you have created your remarketing lists, you need to add a small snippet of code, called the remarketing tag, to your website or app.

This tag helps track user interactions and enables Google Ads to build and update your remarketing lists based on user behavior.

- ➤ Creating Remarketing Campaigns: After setting up your remarketing lists, you can create dedicated remarketing campaigns in Google Ads. These campaigns allow you to define the targeting options, ad formats, bidding strategies, and ad creative that you want to use for remarketing purposes.

- ➤ Tailoring Ad Content: It's important to create compelling and relevant ad content for your remarketing campaigns. Customize your ads based on the user's previous interactions, such as displaying the specific products they viewed or offering exclusive discounts to encourage conversions. This level of personalization helps capture the user's attention and increases the likelihood of engagement.

- ➤ Setting Bid Strategies: Remarketing campaigns offer various bidding options. You can choose to manually set bids or leverage automated bidding strategies like Target CPA (Cost Per Acquisition) or Target ROAS (Return on Ad Spend) to optimize your ad performance. These strategies adjust your bids in real-time based on factors like user intent, device, and location.

➢ Expanding Reach with Similar Audiences: In addition to targeting your existing remarketing lists, you can also leverage Google's Similar Audiences feature. This feature identifies users who share similar characteristics and behavior with your existing remarketing lists, allowing you to expand your reach and target new potential customers.

➢ Analyzing and Optimizing: Regularly monitor the performance of your remarketing campaigns and make data-driven optimizations. Analyze key metrics such as click-through rate (CTR), conversion rate, and return on ad spend (ROAS) to understand the effectiveness of your ads. Adjust your targeting, ad messaging, and bidding strategies to maximize the impact of your remarketing efforts.

By understanding remarketing and implementing it effectively in your Google Ads campaigns, you can stay top-of-mind with your target audience, drive repeat visits, and increase conversions. It's a valuable tool for maximizing the impact of your advertising budget and boosting your overall marketing efforts.

B. Creating Remarketing Lists

Creating remarketing lists is an essential strategy in Google Ads that allows advertisers to target and engage with users who have previously interacted with their website or mobile app. Remarketing lists help to increase brand awareness, drive conversions, and improve overall campaign performance. Let's explore the process of creating remarketing lists step by step:

1. Set up Google Ads and Analytics: To create remarketing lists, you'll need to have Google Ads and Google Analytics accounts linked together. Ensure that the Google Analytics tracking code is correctly implemented on your website or app.

2. Define your remarketing goals: Determine your campaign objectives and what actions you want users to take. It could be encouraging users to complete a purchase, filling out a form, or any other desired conversion.

3. Identify remarketing audiences: Consider which audience segments you want to target based on their past interactions with your website or app. You can create lists for various scenarios, such as all website visitors, specific product page visitors, cart abandoners, or users who completed a specific conversion action.

4. Choose a remarketing method: Google Ads offers several methods to create remarketing lists:

a. Standard remarketing: Targets users who have visited your website or app and displays relevant ads to them as they browse other websites and apps on the Google Display Network.

b. Dynamic remarketing: Especially useful for e-commerce websites, this method shows personalized ads featuring the specific products or services that users viewed on your site.

c. Remarketing lists for search ads (RLSA): With RLSA, you can customize your search ad campaigns and bids for users who have already visited your site. This allows you to tailor your message and bidding strategy for more targeted engagement.

d. Customer Match: This method enables you to upload your own customer data, such as email addresses, and serve ads to those specific individuals when they're signed in to their Google accounts.

e. Video remarketing: Targets users who have interacted with your YouTube videos or YouTube channel and displays ads to them while they watch other videos on the platform.

f. App remarketing: Focuses on engaging users who have already installed your mobile app. You can encourage them to take specific in-app actions or re-engage with the app.

5. Create remarketing lists in Google Ads: Depending on the chosen method, navigate to the "Audience" section in Google Ads, and select "Remarketing Lists." Follow the prompts to create a new list and configure the settings based on your audience criteria.

6. Set list membership duration: Specify how long users should remain on your remarketing list after their last interaction with your website or app. You can choose predefined durations or set a custom duration based on your campaign goals.

7. Customize ad messaging and targeting: Craft compelling ad creatives that resonate with your remarketing audience. Tailor your messaging to address their specific needs, highlight the value of your offerings, or provide incentives to encourage conversions. Additionally, consider adjusting bids, ad placements, or other targeting options to optimize your campaign for remarketing lists.

7. **Monitor and optimize performance**: Continuously monitor the performance of your remarketing campaigns using Google Ads and Analytics. Track key metrics such as impressions, clicks, conversions, and cost per conversion.

Use this data to refine your targeting, adjust bids, and experiment with different ad formats to improve results over time.

Creating remarketing lists in Google Ads allows you to engage with users who have already shown interest in your business, maximizing the chances of conversion. By delivering relevant and personalized ads, you can significantly enhance the effectiveness of your advertising efforts. Remember to comply with privacy policies and regulations while implementing remarketing strategies.

C. Audience targeting options

Audience targeting options in Google Ads refer to the various ways advertisers can reach their desired audience based on specific characteristics and behaviors. These targeting options help advertisers maximize the effectiveness of their ad campaigns by delivering their messages to the right people at the right time. Let's explore some of the key audience targeting options available in Google Ads:

1. **Demographic Targeting**: Advertisers can target audiences based on demographic attributes such as age, gender, parental status, and household income. This allows advertisers to tailor their ads to specific segments of the

population that are most likely to be interested in their products or services.

2. **Location Targeting**: With location targeting, advertisers can specify the geographic locations where they want their ads to be shown. This can be as broad as targeting an entire country or as specific as targeting a particular city or even a radius around a specific address. Location targeting helps businesses reach customers in their target markets and exclude irrelevant locations.

3. **Interest-based Targeting**: Google Ads provides interest-based targeting options that allow advertisers to reach users based on their demonstrated interests and behaviors. These interests are inferred from users' browsing activity, search history, and other online behaviors. Advertisers can select from predefined interest categories or target specific topics relevant to their products or services.

4. **Remarketing**: Remarketing enables advertisers to show ads to users who have previously interacted with their website or mobile app. By placing a remarketing tag or code snippet on their site, advertisers can create custom audience lists and target those users with tailored ads as they browse other websites or use Google services.

5. **In-market Targeting**: In-market targeting allows advertisers to reach users who are actively researching or showing purchase intent for specific products or services. Google identifies users who are actively exploring relevant product categories based on their online behaviors and engagements. This targeting option is particularly useful for businesses looking to capture customers in the consideration phase of the buying process.

6. **Custom Intent Audiences**: Custom intent audiences allow advertisers to define and target specific audiences based on relevant keywords and URLs related to their products or services. Advertisers can create custom intent audiences by entering keywords or URLs that represent the interests or intentions of their desired audience. This option provides more flexibility in reaching potential customers who are actively searching for or consuming content related to the advertiser's offerings.

7. **Similar Audiences**: Similar audiences help advertisers expand their reach by targeting users who have similar characteristics and behaviors to their existing customers. Google Ads analyzes the characteristics and behaviors of an advertiser's remarketing or customer match lists and finds other users who exhibit similar traits. This targeting option is beneficial for reaching new prospects who share commonalities with an advertiser's existing customer base.

8. **Customer Match**: Customer match allows advertisers to target their existing customers by uploading customer email lists to Google Ads. By matching the email addresses with Google user accounts, advertisers can deliver tailored ads to their customer base across Google's platforms. Customer match is useful for upselling, cross-selling, or re-engaging existing customers.

These are just some of the audience targeting options available in Google Ads. Advertisers can combine these options to create highly targeted campaigns and improve their ad performance by reaching the most relevant audience for their business. It's important for advertisers to continually analyze and refine their targeting strategies to optimize their ad campaigns and maximize their return on investment.

CHAPTER TEN: OPTIMIZING CAMPAIGNS FOR MOBILE DEVICES

A. Mobile-specific ad strategies

Mobile-specific ad strategies are essential in today's digital landscape, where mobile devices play a significant role in consumers' lives. To effectively reach and engage with mobile users, businesses need to optimize their Google Ads campaigns specifically for mobile devices. Here, I will explain extensively on mobile-specific ad strategies that can help businesses maximize their mobile advertising efforts.

> - Responsive Design: Creating mobile-responsive ads is crucial for delivering a seamless user experience across various screen sizes and devices. Responsive design ensures that your ads adapt and display correctly on mobile devices, preventing any layout or formatting issues. By using responsive ads, you can reach users on both smartphones and tablets without the need to create separate ad campaigns for each device.

> - Ad Extensions: Take advantage of ad extensions to enhance the visibility and relevance of your mobile ads. Ad extensions provide additional information and features to your ad, making it more useful and engaging for mobile users.

Some popular ad extensions for mobile include call extensions, location extensions, and sitelink extensions. These extensions allow users to call your business directly, find your nearest location, or navigate to specific pages on your website, respectively.

➢ Mobile-Optimized Landing Pages: Once users click on your mobile ad, they should be directed to a mobile-optimized landing page that offers a seamless browsing experience. Ensure that your landing pages load quickly and are designed to be mobile-friendly. Optimize the layout, font sizes, and button placements to make it easy for users to navigate and take desired actions. A well-optimized landing page helps improve user engagement, conversions, and overall campaign performance.

➢ Location Targeting: Mobile devices are inherently tied to users' physical locations, and leveraging location targeting can be an effective mobile-specific ad strategy. By targeting specific geographic areas or using location-based bid adjustments, you can reach users who are nearby or searching for products/services in a particular location. Location targeting is particularly useful for businesses with brick-and-mortar stores or those offering location-specific services.

➢ Mobile App Advertising: Mobile apps are immensely popular, and advertising within relevant mobile apps can be a powerful strategy to reach mobile users.

Google Ads offers various app-specific ad formats, such as mobile app install ads and app engagement ads. These ads can help businesses promote their mobile apps, drive installations, and encourage users to take specific in-app actions. Mobile app advertising can be particularly beneficial for businesses that have a mobile app or offer app-based services.

➢ Video and Visual Ads: Mobile devices offer an immersive multimedia experience, and incorporating video and visual ads can be highly impactful. Create compelling video ads or visually appealing image ads that capture users' attention and deliver your message effectively. Optimize the video ads for mobile viewing by keeping them concise, engaging, and using subtitles or captions for better comprehension without sound. Visual ads should be visually appealing and optimized for quick loading on mobile devices.

➢ Call-Only Campaigns: For businesses that prioritize phone calls as a primary conversion goal, call-only campaigns are an ideal mobile-specific strategy. Call-only campaigns display ads with a "Call" button directly on mobile search results, enabling users to call your business with a single tap. This strategy is particularly effective for service-based businesses like plumbers, electricians, or healthcare providers, where phone calls play a crucial role in generating leads.

➤ Mobile Bid Adjustments: Mobile-specific bid adjustments allow you to fine-tune your ad bids based on the device users are using. Analyze your campaign data to understand the performance differences between mobile, desktop, and tablet devices. If mobile devices are driving better results or have a higher conversion rate, consider increasing your bid adjustments for mobile to increase the visibility of your ads and capture more mobile traffic.

➤ App Deep Linking: If your business has a mobile app, leverage app deep linking to provide a seamless user experience. Deep linking allows you to direct users to specific pages within your app from your mobile ads. By utilizing deep links, you can guide users to relevant content or specific actions within your app, increasing user engagement and conversions. Deep linking can be particularly useful for e-commerce businesses, where you can deep link users to product pages or offer exclusive in-app promotions.

➤ Mobile Remarketing: Implementing mobile remarketing campaigns is a valuable strategy to re-engage users who have previously interacted with your brand on mobile devices.

By using mobile-specific remarketing lists, you can deliver personalized ads to users who have visited your mobile site or app. This helps reinforce your brand message, remind users of products or services they showed interest in, and encourage them to take further action.

➤ Ad Scheduling: Understanding the time of day when mobile users are most active and receptive to ads can significantly impact your campaign's success. Utilize ad scheduling to adjust your mobile ad visibility based on peak user activity periods. By aligning your ads with the most optimal times, you can increase the chances of capturing users' attention and driving conversions. Analyze your campaign data to identify patterns and trends in mobile user behavior to inform your ad scheduling decisions.

➤ Mobile-Specific Ad Copy: Crafting compelling ad copy that speaks directly to mobile users is essential for maximizing your mobile ad performance. Keep your ad copy concise, clear, and tailored to the mobile user's context. Highlight the key benefits or unique selling points of your products or services in a concise manner. Incorporate strong and action-oriented language to encourage users to take immediate action, such as "Shop Now," "Call Now," or "Download the App."

➢ Continuous Optimization and Testing: Mobile advertising landscape and user behavior are constantly evolving. It's crucial to continuously monitor and optimize your mobile ad campaigns. Regularly review your campaign data, including click-through rates, conversion rates, and engagement metrics, to identify areas for improvement. A/B test different ad formats, visuals, headlines, and calls-to-action to determine which variations resonate best with your mobile audience. Use the insights gained from testing to refine your strategies and optimize campaign performance.

Overall, mobile-specific ad strategies are vital for businesses aiming to effectively target and engage with mobile users. By implementing responsive design, utilizing ad extensions, optimizing landing pages, leveraging location targeting, exploring mobile app advertising, incorporating video and visual ads, and employing other mobile-specific tactics, businesses can enhance their mobile ad performance, increase user engagement, and drive conversions. Continual optimization, testing, and staying abreast of the evolving mobile landscape are key to achieving long-term success in mobile advertising.

B. Responsive ads and mobile site optimization

Responsive ads and mobile site optimization are crucial aspects of a successful Google Ads campaign, especially in today's mobile-driven world. In this response, I will explain these concepts in detail.

➤ Responsive Ads:

Responsive ads are a versatile ad format that automatically adjusts its size, appearance, and format to fit various ad spaces across the Google Display Network (GDN). They provide an optimal viewing experience for users, whether they are browsing on desktops, tablets, or mobile devices.

Benefits of Responsive Ads:

- Improved reach: With responsive ads, you can reach a broader audience by automatically adapting to different ad placements and screen sizes.
- Time and resource efficiency: Instead of creating multiple ad sizes, you can create one responsive ad, saving time and effort in ad creation.
- Optimization potential: Responsive ads utilize Google's machine learning algorithms to optimize performance by automatically testing different combinations of headlines, images, and text to find the most effective ad variations.

Creating Responsive Ads:

To create responsive ads, you need to provide multiple assets, including headlines, images, descriptions, and logos. Google Ads will then dynamically combine these assets to generate ad variations. It's essential to follow best practices when creating responsive ads, such as:

- Including at least one landscape and one square image to accommodate different placements.
- Writing compelling headlines and descriptions that work well together and make sense when combined in different ways.
- Using a clear logo that represents your brand effectively.

➢ **Mobile Site Optimization:**

Mobile site optimization refers to the process of optimizing your website to provide the best possible user experience for mobile visitors. As the majority of internet users access the web through mobile devices, it's crucial to ensure that your website is mobile-friendly and performs well on smaller screens.

Key Aspects of Mobile Site Optimization:

- Responsive design: Implement a responsive web design that automatically adapts to different screen sizes and orientations. This ensures that your website appears correctly on any mobile device.

- Fast page load speed: Mobile users have limited patience for slow-loading websites. Optimize your website's performance by minimizing file sizes, leveraging browser caching, and compressing images to reduce load times.
- Clear and concise content: Mobile users tend to have shorter attention spans, so make sure your content is concise, easy to read, and formatted appropriately for mobile screens. Use shorter paragraphs, bullet points, and clear headings to improve readability.
- Mobile-friendly navigation: Simplify your website's navigation menu and ensure that it is easy to use on touch screens. Implement mobile-specific features like a sticky header or a hamburger menu to optimize the user experience.
- Call-to-action optimization: Make sure your call-to-action buttons are prominent, easy to tap, and clearly communicate the desired action. Optimize their placement and size to ensure they are accessible on smaller screens.

Mobile site optimization not only improves the user experience but also contributes to better ad performance. If your website is mobile-friendly, users are more likely to engage with your ads and convert into customers.

CHAPTER ELEVEN: LOCAL ADVERTISING WITH GOOGLE ADS

A. Setting up local Campaigns

Setting up local campaigns in Google Ads is a great way to target specific geographic areas and reach potential customers who are located near your business. With local campaigns, you can promote your products or services to people who are searching for them on Google or using Google Maps.

To get started with setting up a local campaign, follow these steps:

1. **Campaign creation**: Sign in to your Google Ads account and click on the "Campaigns" tab. Then, click on the blue plus button to create a new campaign. Choose the goal that aligns with your business objectives, such as "Sales," "Leads," or "Website Traffic."

2. **Campaign type selection**: Select the "Local Campaign" option under the "Campaign type" section. This will ensure that your campaign is optimized for local targeting.

3. **Business location**: Provide your business address or multiple locations if applicable. This will help Google Ads identify the geographic area you want to target with your campaign.

4. **Campaign settings**: Set your campaign name, budget, and bidding strategy. It's recommended to start with a modest budget and monitor performance before scaling up.

5. **Ad format**: Create compelling ad formats that resonate with your target audience. Local campaigns support various ad formats, including responsive search ads, image ads, and dynamic ads. Ensure your ad copy highlights the unique selling points of your business and includes relevant keywords.

6. **Ad extensions**: Take advantage of ad extensions to provide additional information about your business, such as phone numbers, location addresses, or links to specific pages on your website. This can enhance the visibility and appeal of your ads.

7. **Location targeting**: Specify the geographic area where you want your ads to appear. You can choose specific locations, radius targeting, or even target by zip codes.

8. **Language and audience targeting**: Select the preferred language for your ads and define your target audience based on demographics, interests, or behaviors. This helps narrow down your campaign's reach to people who are most likely to be interested in your offerings.

9. **Measurement and tracking**: Implement conversion tracking to measure the effectiveness of your local campaign. Set up conversion actions, such as form submissions, phone calls, or purchases, and place the tracking code on relevant pages of your website.

10. **Optimization and monitoring**: Regularly monitor the performance of your local campaign. Make adjustments to your bidding, ad copy, and targeting settings based on the insights you gather. Consider using local-specific keywords to increase relevancy and improve click-through rates.

In addition to these steps, it's essential to continuously optimize your local campaign. Test different ad variations, track conversions, and adjust your targeting settings to maximize your results. By setting up local campaigns effectively, you can connect with potential customers who are actively searching for products or services in your area, driving more foot traffic and leads to your business.

B. Location targeting options

Location targeting options in Google Ads allow advertisers to define the specific geographic locations where their ads should be shown. By targeting the right locations, advertisers can effectively reach their desired audience and maximize the performance of their campaigns. Google Ads offers several location targeting options that provide flexibility and control over where ads are displayed. These options include:

➤ Geographic Location Targeting: This option allows advertisers to target ads based on countries, regions, cities, or even specific areas within a city. Advertisers can select multiple locations or exclude certain areas to refine their targeting.

➤ Radius Targeting: With this option, advertisers can target a specific radius around a particular location. They can choose the center point, such as a store or office address, and set a radius, for example, 10 miles. Ads will be shown to users within that radius, ensuring a localized reach.

➤ Location Groups: Google Ads offers predefined location groups, such as airports, universities, or shopping centers, to target specific types of locations. Advertisers can select these groups to reach users who are likely to be present in those locations.

➢ Demographics and Affinity: In addition to geographic targeting, Google Ads provides options to target ads based on demographic information, such as age, gender, and household income. Advertisers can also target audiences with specific interests or affinities, allowing for more precise targeting.

➢ Exclusions: Advertisers can exclude specific locations where they don't want their ads to be shown. This helps prevent wasted ad spend on irrelevant or low-performing locations.

➢ Customization: Google Ads allows advertisers to create custom targeting by uploading location lists or importing location data through the Google My Business account. This enables businesses to reach specific areas not covered by predefined options.

➢ Advanced Location Options: Google Ads provides additional advanced location options, such as location-based bid adjustments. Advertisers can increase or decrease bids for specific locations based on their performance or strategic importance.

When setting up location targeting, it's important to consider the target audience, campaign objectives, and the geographic reach of the business. Advertisers can analyze data from previous campaigns, leverage insights from Google Analytics, or conduct market research to identify the most relevant and effective locations to target. By using the appropriate location targeting options in Google Ads, advertisers can enhance the relevance of their ads, improve click-through rates, increase conversions, and ultimately drive better results for their advertising campaigns.

C. Google My Business integration

Google My Business integration refers to the process of connecting your Google My Business (GMB) account with your Google Ads account. This integration allows you to enhance your online advertising efforts by leveraging the power of your GMB listing. When properly integrated, your GMB information can be synchronized with your Google Ads campaigns, providing several benefits for your business.

First and foremost, integrating Google My Business with Google Ads enables you to display location extensions in your ads. Location extensions include important details about your business, such as the address, phone number, and map directions. These extensions make your ads more relevant and useful to potential customers, as they can easily find and contact your business directly from the ad. This integration is especially valuable for businesses with physical locations, as it helps drive foot traffic and increase store visits.

Moreover, integrating Google My Business and Google Ads allows you to access additional ad formats. One notable example is the Local Campaigns feature, which is specifically designed to drive store visits and promote businesses with physical locations. Local Campaigns leverage data from your GMB listing, such as store hours and location, to automatically optimize your ads and maximize local reach. By utilizing this integration, you can effectively target nearby customers who are actively searching for products or services like yours.

Another advantage of Google My Business integration is the ability to track and measure the performance of your GMB listing alongside your Google Ads campaigns. Through Google Ads, you gain insights into important metrics like impressions, clicks, and conversions associated with your GMB profile. This integration allows you to assess the impact of your GMB listing on your advertising efforts and make data-driven decisions to optimize your overall marketing strategy.

Additionally, integrating Google My Business and Google Ads enables you to take advantage of Smart Bidding strategies.

Smart Bidding utilizes machine learning algorithms to automatically optimize your bids for maximum conversion value or conversion volume. By linking your GMB account, you can utilize location-specific signals and performance data to enhance the effectiveness of Smart Bidding. This integration helps you achieve better results and maximize the return on your advertising investment.

To integrate Google My Business with Google Ads, you need to follow a few steps. First, ensure that you have both a Google My Business account and a Google Ads account. Then, link these accounts by signing in to your Google Ads account, navigating to the "Tools & Settings" menu, selecting "Linked accounts," and choosing "Google My Business." Follow the instructions provided to complete the integration process.

Overall, integrating Google My Business with Google Ads offers several advantages for businesses. It allows you to display location extensions, access additional ad formats like Local Campaigns, track performance metrics, and leverage Smart Bidding strategies. By synchronizing your GMB information with your Google Ads campaigns, you can enhance your online advertising presence, drive more relevant traffic to your business, and achieve better results overall.

CHAPTER TWELVE: ADVANCED GOOGLE ADS STRATEGIES

A. Ad Scheduling and Dayparting

Ad scheduling, also known as dayparting, is a feature in Google Ads that allows advertisers to control when their ads are shown to potential customers. It enables advertisers to target specific days and times of the week when their target audience is more likely to be active and engaged. By leveraging ad scheduling, advertisers can optimize their ad campaigns to reach their desired audience at the most opportune moments. Here's how it works:

Accessing Ad Scheduling: Ad scheduling is accessible within the Google Ads platform. Advertisers can navigate to the campaign settings and select the "Ad Schedule" tab to set up their preferred scheduling parameters.

1. **Setting up ad schedules**: Advertisers can define the days and times during which they want their ads to be displayed. They can choose specific days of the week or select all days. Similarly, they can specify precise times or choose entire time blocks for their ad visibility.

2. **Bidding adjustments**: Ad scheduling also allows advertisers to make bid adjustments based on specific days and times. This feature enables advertisers to increase or decrease their bids during peak or off-peak periods, ensuring

they maximize their ad visibility during high-conversion times.

3. **Performance analysis**: After implementing ad scheduling, advertisers can analyze the performance of their ads during different time segments. Google Ads provides data on impressions, clicks, conversions, and other relevant metrics broken down by day and time. This information helps advertisers identify patterns and trends to optimize their scheduling strategy further.

Benefits of Ad Scheduling:

1. Cost efficiency: Ad scheduling helps advertisers allocate their budgets effectively by showing ads only during periods when their target audience is most likely to engage. By avoiding low-conversion periods, advertisers can optimize their spending and reduce wasted ad impressions.

2. Targeting relevance: Ad scheduling allows advertisers to align their ad displays with the behavior and preferences of their target audience. They can ensure their ads are visible during the times when their potential customers are actively searching for products or services, increasing the likelihood of conversions.

3. Increased campaign performance: By leveraging ad scheduling, advertisers can focus their advertising efforts during peak times, where there is higher competition and potential for increased conversions. This strategy can lead to improved campaign performance, higher click-through rates, and better return on investment (ROI).

4. Flexibility and control: Ad scheduling provides advertisers with the flexibility to adjust their campaigns based on their business goals and target audience behavior. They can experiment with different time segments, monitor performance, and make data-driven decisions to refine their scheduling strategy over time.

5. Multi-location targeting: Ad scheduling is particularly valuable for businesses operating in multiple time zones or targeting audiences in different geographical locations. It allows advertisers to customize their schedules for each region, ensuring their ads are displayed at optimal times across various time zones.

Overall, ad scheduling, or dayparting, is a powerful feature in Google Ads that enables advertisers to control when their ads are displayed to their target audience. By strategically choosing the days and times for ad visibility, advertisers can optimize their campaign performance, increase relevance, and improve cost efficiency.

B. Ad Rotation and Testing

Ad rotation and testing are critical components of a successful Google Ads campaign. Ad rotation refers to the way Google displays your ads within an ad group. It determines which ads are shown to users and how often they appear. The primary purpose of ad rotation is to ensure that your ads are optimized for performance and that you're getting the most out of your advertising budget. When it comes to ad rotation, there are different options available, and each option serves a specific purpose. The most common ad rotation settings in Google Ads are:

1. **"Optimize" (formerly known as "Optimize for conversions")**: This setting uses Google's machine learning algorithms to automatically show the ads that are more likely to achieve your campaign's conversion goals. It takes into account various factors, such as ad performance history, user context, and available data to determine which ad is the most relevant and likely to drive conversions. This setting is suitable when you have sufficient conversion data to optimize towards.

2. **"Rotate Indefinitely" (formerly known as "Rotate evenly")**: This setting gives equal visibility to all ads within an ad group. It doesn't prioritize any particular ad and allows them to rotate evenly. This option is useful when you want to test different ad variations and determine which ones perform better based on metrics like click-through rate (CTR)

or conversion rate. However, it's important to note that Google may automatically optimize ad serving based on performance over time, even if this setting is selected.

3. **"Optimize for clicks"**: This setting is similar to the "Optimize" option, but it focuses on maximizing the number of clicks rather than conversions. It's suitable when your primary campaign goal is to drive traffic to your website or landing page rather than specific conversions.

Now, let's dive into ad testing, which goes hand in hand with ad rotation. Ad testing involves creating multiple ad variations within an ad group and analyzing their performance to identify the most effective ads. Here are some key considerations for effective ad testing:

➢ Ad variations: Create multiple ads with different headlines, descriptions, calls to action, or even different ad formats. It's essential to test only one element at a time to isolate the impact of each change and draw meaningful conclusions.

➢ Testing duration: Allow your ads to gather sufficient data before drawing conclusions. The duration depends on the amount of traffic your campaign receives. Ideally, aim for statistical significance, which means having enough data to make statistically valid conclusions.

➤ Performance metrics: Monitor key performance indicators (KPIs) such as CTR, conversion rate, cost per conversion, and return on ad spend (ROAS) to evaluate the performance of each ad variation. Consider using conversion tracking and A/B testing tools to simplify the analysis process.

➤ Iterative testing: Once you identify the winning ad variations, continue testing new ideas to improve performance further. Testing should be an ongoing process to ensure your ads remain relevant and effective over time.

By utilizing different ad rotation settings and conducting systematic ad testing, you can optimize your Google Ads campaigns for better performance, higher click-through rates, improved conversion rates, and ultimately, a higher return on your advertising investment.

C. Advanced targeting and exclusions

Ons in Google Ads allow advertisers to refine their audience targeting and ensure that their ads reach the right people while excluding irrelevant audiences. By using advanced targeting and exclusion techniques, advertisers can optimize their campaigns for better performance and higher return on investment (ROI).

➤ Demographic Targeting: Google Ads offers several demographic targeting options to reach specific audiences based on age, gender, parental status, and household income. This enables advertisers to tailor their ads to the preferences and characteristics of their target audience.

➤ Location Targeting: Advertisers can narrow down their ad's reach by targeting specific geographic locations. This can be done at various levels, such as countries, cities, regions, or even specific radius targeting around a particular location. Location targeting helps businesses focus their advertising efforts on areas where they can generate the most relevant leads or customers.

➤ Device Targeting: With the proliferation of mobile devices, it's crucial for advertisers to optimize their campaigns for different device types. Google Ads allows advertisers to target specific devices, including desktops, tablets, and mobile devices. This feature enables advertisers to customize their ad experiences based on the device used by their target audience.

➤ Custom Intent and In-market Audiences: Custom intent audiences allow advertisers to target users based on their recent search activities and the content they have consumed. This targeting option is ideal for reaching users who are actively researching or showing interest in specific products or services. In-market audiences, on the other hand, target users who are actively considering making a purchase in a particular product or service category. By leveraging these audience types, advertisers can focus their ads on users who are more likely to convert.

➤ Remarketing and Similar Audiences: Remarketing allows advertisers to show ads to users who have previously interacted with their website, app, or YouTube channel. By targeting these past visitors, advertisers can remind them of their products or services, increase brand awareness, and encourage conversions. Google Ads also provides similar audiences, which are groups of users who share characteristics with the advertiser's existing remarketing audience. This feature helps advertisers expand their reach to potential customers who exhibit similar behavior and interests.

➢ Topic and Placement Exclusions: Advertisers can exclude specific topics or placements where they do not want their ads to appear. For example, if an advertiser sells high-end luxury products, they may want to exclude websites or content related to budget or discount shopping. By using topic and placement exclusions, advertisers can ensure that their ads are displayed in relevant and brand-safe environments, improving the overall ad performance and targeting efficiency.

➢ Audience Exclusions: Advertisers can exclude specific audiences from their campaigns to avoid targeting users who are not likely to convert or align with their campaign goals. This can be done by excluding particular demographics, interests, or remarketing audiences. Audience exclusions help advertisers focus their budget and resources on the most valuable and relevant audience segments.

Overall, advanced targeting and exclusions in Google Ads provide advertisers with powerful tools to refine their audience targeting and ensure that their ads are displayed to the right people. By leveraging these features effectively, advertisers can improve campaign performance, increase conversions, and maximize their advertising ROI.

D. Smart Bidding Strategies

Smart Bidding strategies are automated bidding strategies in Google Ads that use machine learning algorithms to optimize your ad bids in real time. These strategies aim to maximize the performance of your campaigns by adjusting bids based on various signals and user behavior.

There are several types of Smart Bidding strategies available in Google Ads, including:

➢ Target CPA (Cost-Per-Acquisition): This strategy sets bids to help you get as many conversions as possible at or below your specified target cost per acquisition. It uses historical data to predict the likelihood of a conversion and adjusts bids accordingly.

➢ Target ROAS (Return On Advertising Spend): With this strategy, you set a target return on ad spend (ROAS), and the algorithm adjusts your bids to maximize conversion value while reaching that target. It takes into account factors such as conversion rates and the value of each conversion.

➢ Maximize Conversions: This strategy aims to get you the maximum number of conversions within your budget. The algorithm automatically sets bids to drive as many conversions as possible. It works well when you don't have specific cost or revenue targets.

➢ Enhanced CPC (Cost-Per-Click): This strategy automatically adjusts your manual bids in real time based on the likelihood of a conversion. It increases bids for clicks that are more likely to lead to conversions and reduces bids for less valuable clicks.

➢ Maximize Clicks: This strategy focuses on driving as many clicks as possible within your budget. The algorithm automatically sets bids to maximize the number of clicks your ads receive.

➢ Target Impression Share: This strategy helps you achieve a specific impression share goal for your ads. You can choose to target the absolute top of the page, the top of the page, or anywhere on the page. The algorithm adjusts bids to increase the chances of your ads appearing in the desired position.

➢ Smart Bidding strategies take into account a wide range of signals, such as device, location, time of day, remarketing lists, and more. They continuously learn and adapt to optimize your bidding decisions and improve campaign performance. It's important to have sufficient historical conversion data for Smart Bidding to work effectively.

> ➤ When using Smart Bidding, it's crucial to monitor your campaigns regularly and make necessary adjustments. Smart Bidding strategies provide automation and efficiency, but human oversight is still needed to ensure the bidding aligns with your business goals and performance targets.

Overall, Smart Bidding strategies in Google Ads leverage machine learning to automate bidding decisions and optimize campaign performance. They offer a range of options to suit different advertising goals and can help you achieve better results by adjusting bids in real time based on various signals and historical data.

CHAPTER THIRTEEN: TROUBLESHOOTING AND OPTIMIZATION TIPS

A. Common Issues and Solutions

Common Issues and Solutions in Google Ads

1. **Low Click-Through Rate (CTR):**
   - Issue: Your ads may have a low CTR, which means they are not generating enough clicks.

   - Solution: Improve your ad relevance and quality by optimizing your ad copy and using relevant keywords. Test different ad variations to find what resonates best with your audience. Consider refining your targeting to reach a more relevant audience.

2. **High Cost-Per-Click (CPC):**
   - Issue: Your CPC may be higher than anticipated, resulting in increased advertising costs.

- Solution: Review your keyword bids and adjust them to ensure they align with your budget. Refine your keyword targeting to focus on more specific and relevant keywords. Improve your Quality Score by enhancing ad

  relevance and landing page experience, as a higher Quality Score can lead to lower CPCs.

3. **Low Conversion Rate**:
   - Issue: You may be receiving a significant number of clicks, but they are not converting into desired actions (such as sales or sign-ups).

   - Solution: Evaluate your landing page to ensure it is user-friendly, mobile-optimized, and provides a clear call-to-action. Make sure your landing page aligns with the messaging in your ads. Test different variations of landing pages to optimize conversion rates. Consider implementing conversion tracking and analyze the data to identify bottlenecks.

4. **Limited Ad Visibility**:
   - Issue: Your ads may not be appearing as frequently as desired, reducing your visibility and potential reach.

- Solution: Increase your bids to improve your ad rank and increase visibility. Optimize your ad scheduling to display ads during peak hours or when your target audience is most active. Expand your targeting options to include relevant keywords, placements, or audiences.

  Ensure your daily budget is sufficient to support your campaign goals.

5. **Ad Disapprovals or Policy Violations**:
   - Issue: Your ads may be disapproved or flagged for policy violations, preventing them from running.

   - Solution: Carefully review Google Ads policies and guidelines to understand the specific violation. Make necessary adjustments to your ad copy, landing page content, or targeting to comply with the policies. If uncertain, reach out to Google Ads support for clarification or assistance.

6. **Irrelevant Ad Impressions**:
   - Issue: Your ads may be receiving impressions from irrelevant searches or placements, wasting your ad budget.

- Solution: Refine your keyword targeting by using negative keywords to exclude irrelevant search terms. Monitor your ad placements and exclude any websites or apps that generate low-quality traffic. Regularly review your campaign's performance and make necessary adjustments to improve relevancy.

7. **Poor Ad Position**:
   - Issue: Your ads may consistently appear in lower positions, resulting in lower visibility and potentially reduced performance.

   - Solution: Increase your keyword bids to improve ad rank and secure higher positions. Improve your Quality Score by optimizing ad relevance, landing page experience, and expected click-through rate. Consider adjusting your targeting options or using bid adjustments to target higher-converting segments of your audience.

8. **Limited Budget**:
   - Issue: Your campaign may be limited by a small budget, preventing you from maximizing your advertising potential.

   - Solution: Evaluate your campaign performance and prioritize the most effective keywords, ad groups, or campaigns. Consider increasing your budget to reach a larger audience and generate more conversions. Implement automated bidding strategies to optimize your budget allocation and maximize results within your budget limitations.

Remember to regularly monitor and analyze your Google Ads performance, utilize available data and insights to make informed decisions, and continuously test and refine your strategies to improve your overall campaign effectiveness.

B. Campaign Optimization Techniques

Campaign optimization techniques refer to the strategies and practices used to improve the performance and effectiveness of Google Ads campaigns. These techniques aim to maximize the return on investment (ROI) and achieve specific campaign goals, such as increasing conversions, driving more traffic, or improving ad relevance. Here are some key campaign optimization techniques:

1. **Keyword Optimization**: Conduct thorough keyword research to identify relevant and high-performing keywords for your campaign. Continuously monitor and refine your keyword list to include valuable keywords and exclude irrelevant or low-performing ones. Regularly update your

match types (broad, phrase, exact) to fine-tune your targeting.

2. **Ad Copy Optimization:** Create compelling and relevant ad copies that align with your target audience's needs and intent. Test different variations of headlines, descriptions, and calls-

to-action (CTAs) to identify the most effective combinations. Use ad extensions to enhance your ads and improve visibility.

3. **Landing Page Optimization**: Ensure that your landing pages provide a seamless and engaging user experience. Optimize landing page load times, make the content relevant to the ad copy, and ensure clear and prominent CTAs. Conduct A/B tests to identify the best-performing landing page design and layout.

4. **Ad Scheduling and Bid Adjustments**: Analyze your campaign performance data to identify the most profitable times of day or days of the week. Adjust your ad scheduling and bid adjustments to increase or decrease bids during these high-converting periods, maximizing your ad's visibility and budget allocation.

5. **Geographic Targeting**: Refine your targeting by focusing on the locations that generate the most conversions or valuable traffic. Use location bid adjustments to allocate higher bids for regions with higher performance and lower bids for regions with lower performance.

6. **Device Targeting**: Analyze the performance of your ads on different devices (desktop, mobile, tablet) and adjust bids accordingly. Optimize your landing pages for mobile devices to ensure a seamless experience.

7. **Ad Placement Optimization**: Review the performance of your ads on the Google Display Network and make adjustments to maximize visibility on high-performing placements. Use placement exclusions to avoid displaying your ads on irrelevant or low-quality websites.

8. **Conversion Tracking and Measurement**: Set up conversion tracking to measure the success of your campaigns. Identify which keywords, ads, and targeting options are driving the most conversions. Use this data to optimize your campaign elements and allocate your budget effectively.

9. **Ad Testing**: Continuously test different ad variations to identify the most effective combinations. Test different

headlines, descriptions, CTAs, and even ad formats to find the best-performing ads. Regularly review your testing results and make data-driven decisions.

10. **Audience Targeting**: Leverage audience targeting options such as demographic targeting, remarketing, or similar audiences to reach specific groups of users who are more likely to convert. Monitor the performance of your audience segments and adjust bids or tailor your messaging accordingly.

Remember, campaign optimization is an ongoing process. Regularly monitor your campaign's performance, analyze data, and make data-driven adjustments to improve your ad performance and achieve your campaign goals.

C. Ad policy Compliance

Ad Policy Compliance refers to the adherence to the rules and guidelines set by Google Ads to ensure that advertisements meet specific standards and requirements. It is crucial for advertisers to understand and comply with these policies to prevent their ads from being disapproved or their accounts from being suspended.

Google Ads has a comprehensive set of policies that cover various aspects of advertising, including content, landing pages, ad formats, and user experience. These policies are designed to maintain a safe and positive user experience by promoting transparency, relevance, and quality in ads.

To achieve ad policy compliance, advertisers should pay attention to the following key areas:

➢ Prohibited Content: Google Ads prohibits the promotion of certain content, such as illegal products or services, counterfeit goods, dangerous substances, and discriminatory content. Advertisers must ensure that their ads do not violate these content guidelines.

➢ Misleading or Deceptive Practices: Ads must provide accurate and truthful information to users. Misleading claims, deceptive practices, or false advertising are strictly prohibited. Advertisers should clearly represent their products or services and avoid any tactics that may mislead or confuse users.

➢ Unacceptable Business Practices: Google Ads restricts ads that promote unethical or non-compliant business practices, such as deceptive behavior, unauthorized collection of personal information, or the sale of counterfeit goods. Advertisers must comply with legal and ethical standards in their advertising practices.

➤ User Safety and Privacy: Ads must respect user privacy and ensure a safe browsing experience. Google Ads prohibits the use of spyware, malware, or any tactics that compromise user safety or security. Advertisers should

also handle user data responsibly and adhere to applicable data protection laws.

➤ Landing Page Quality: The landing page that users are directed to after clicking an ad should provide a positive user experience and be relevant to the ad content. Advertisers should ensure that their landing pages load quickly, contain original content, and are easy to navigate.

➤ Restricted Content: Certain types of content are restricted and require additional approvals or certifications before they can be advertised. This includes alcohol, gambling, healthcare-related products or services, and financial services. Advertisers should review the specific policies for each restricted category and comply with the additional requirements.

To maintain ad policy compliance, it is essential for advertisers to regularly review their ads, landing pages, and business practices. Google Ads provides resources, including the Policy Center and the Policy Help Center, to assist advertisers in understanding and complying with the ad policies.

Failure to comply with ad policies can result in ads being disapproved, account suspension, or even permanent bans. Advertisers should take proactive measures to ensure their ads meet the policy requirements and promote a positive user experience.

CHAPTER FOURTEEN: KEEPING UP WITH GOOGLE ADS UPDATES

A. Staying informed about Google Ads changes

Staying informed about Google Ads changes is crucial for anyone running advertising campaigns on the platform. Google frequently updates and introduces new features, tools, and policies that can significantly impact your ad performance and overall campaign success.

To ensure you stay ahead of these changes, here are some key strategies:

1. **Google Ads Official Sources**: Google provides several official channels to communicate updates. Stay connected with the Google Ads blog (ads.googleblog.com) and the Google Ads Help Center (support.google.com/google-ads) for the latest news, feature announcements, best practices, and policy updates. These sources are reliable and offer detailed information directly from Google.

2. **Google Ads Notifications**: Google Ads platform offers in-platform notifications to alert advertisers about significant

changes and updates. Make sure you have enabled notifications within your account settings to receive important messages and announcements directly.

3. **Google Ads Email Updates**: Google occasionally sends email updates to advertisers regarding new features, changes in policies, and industry trends. Keep an eye on your inbox for these messages and ensure they are not going to your spam folder.

4. **Google Ads Academy**: The Google Ads Academy (ads.google.com/academy) provides a wealth of educational resources, including training courses, webinars, and certifications. By participating in these programs, you can stay informed about the latest updates, learn about new features, and gain insights into best practices for successful advertising on Google Ads.

5. **Google Ads Community**: Engage with the Google Ads Community (support.google.com/google-ads/community) to connect with other advertisers, ask questions, and stay up-to-date with the latest industry discussions. The community is a valuable resource for learning from experienced advertisers and industry experts.

6. **Google Marketing Live**: Google hosts an annual event called Google Marketing Live, where they announce major updates, new features, and product launches. Follow this event to get a comprehensive overview of upcoming changes and industry trends. You can watch the live stream or access recorded sessions afterward.

7. **Industry News and Blogs**: Keep up with reputable industry news websites, blogs, and forums that cover Google Ads updates. Websites like Search Engine Land, Search Engine Journal, and PPC Hero often provide insightful articles, analysis, and expert opinions on the latest changes and trends in the advertising industry.

8. **Google Ads Experiments and Betas**: Google frequently tests new features and updates through its Experiments and Betas programs. Keep an eye out for invitations to participate in these programs, as they give you the opportunity to try out new features and provide feedback directly to Google.

By utilizing these strategies and staying informed about Google Ads changes, you can adapt your advertising strategies, leverage new features, and ensure your campaigns remain effective and successful in an ever-evolving digital advertising landscape.

B. Best Practices for Adapting to Updates

Best practices for adapting to updates in Google Ads involve staying informed, being proactive, and continuously optimizing your campaigns.

Here's a concise explanation of these best practices:

➤ Stay informed: It's crucial to keep up with the latest updates and changes in Google Ads. Regularly check the Google Ads Help Center, official blogs, and community forums to stay informed about new features, policy changes, and best practices. Following Google's official social media channels and attending webinars can also provide valuable insights.

➤ Be proactive: When updates are announced, take proactive steps to understand the impact they may have on your campaigns. Read the documentation and guidelines provided by Google and assess how the changes might affect your targeting, bidding strategies, ad formats, or landing page requirements.

➤ Review performance data: Analyze your campaign performance before and after updates to understand the effects. Look for any changes in key metrics such as click-through rate (CTR), conversion rate, cost per conversion, and overall campaign performance. Identify areas that may require adjustments or optimization.

➤ Test and experiment: Test different strategies and approaches to adapt to updates effectively. Conduct A/B testing with ad copy variations, landing page optimizations, bid adjustments, or new targeting options. By testing small-scale changes and measuring their impact, you can determine the most effective tactics for your specific campaigns.

➤ Maintain relevance: Updates often aim to improve user experience and ad relevance. Focus on aligning your ad campaigns with the intent of your target audience. Ensure that your keywords, ad copy, and landing pages are highly relevant to the user's search query and deliver a consistent message throughout the conversion funnel.

➤ Leverage new features: Updates often introduce new features and tools that can enhance your campaign performance. Explore and experiment with these features to maximize your ad reach and engage with your audience more effectively. Examples include responsive search ads, Smart Bidding strategies, audience targeting options, and ad extensions.

➢ Monitor policy changes: Stay vigilant about policy updates to avoid any violations that could lead to ad disapprovals or account suspensions. Regularly review

the advertising policies and guidelines provided by Google to ensure compliance. If updates impact your existing campaigns, make the necessary adjustments to maintain policy adherence.

Remember, adapting to updates in Google Ads is an ongoing process. Continuously monitor your campaigns, stay informed, and iterate based on data and performance to achieve optimal results.

CHAPTER FIFTEEN: CONCLUSION

The Essential Google Ads Guide provides valuable insights into maximizing the potential of Google Ads campaigns. The key points to remember from this book are:

Keyword Research: Thorough keyword research is crucial to identify relevant and high-performing keywords for your ads. Use tools like Google Keyword Planner to discover keywords with adequate search volume and low competition. This helps you target the right audience and increase the chances of your ads appearing in relevant search results.

Ad Creation: Crafting compelling and relevant ad copies is crucial to capture the attention of your target audience. Your ad should clearly convey your unique value proposition and stand out from your competitors. Highlight unique selling points, include incorporation of strong and persuasive calls-to-action that encourage users to click on your ad. Additionally, make use of ad extensions such as sitelinks, call extensions, and structured snippets to enhance the visibility and engagement of your ads.

Campaign Structure: Properly structuring your campaigns is vital for organizing your ads effectively. Create well-organized ad groups that group together similar keywords and ads.

This improves the relevance of your ads and ensures that they are shown to users searching for specific keywords. Utilize ad scheduling to control when your ads are shown and optimize your budget allocation. Location targeting allows you to target specific geographic locations where your target audience is located.

Bid Management: Bidding strategically is crucial for achieving your advertising goals within your allocated budget. You can choose between automated bidding strategies, which leverage machine learning algorithms to optimize your bids automatically, or manual bidding, where you have full control over your bids. Consider factors such as your campaign objectives, historical performance data, and competition when determining your bidding strategy.

Landing Page Optimization: A well-optimized landing page is essential for converting ad clicks into meaningful actions such as purchases, sign-ups, or inquiries. Ensure that your landing page is highly relevant to the ad that users clicked on, providing a seamless and consistent experience. Optimize your landing page for fast loading times, clear and concise messaging, and a prominent call-to-action. A user-friendly and visually appealing design can also positively impact user engagement and conversions.

Tracking and Measurement: Implementing conversion tracking is crucial for understanding the performance of your Google Ads campaigns. By integrating Google Analytics, you gain valuable insights into user behavior, conversion rates, and other key metrics. Regularly analyze the data to identify trends, patterns, and areas for improvement. This data-driven approach enables you to make informed decisions and optimize your campaigns effectively.

Continuous Optimization: Successful Google Ads campaigns require ongoing monitoring and optimization. Regularly review and adjust your campaigns based on their performance. This includes making changes to keywords, ad copies, bids, targeting, and other campaign settings. Conduct A/B testing to experiment with different strategies and identify what works best for your target audience. Continuously testing and refining your campaigns is essential for maximizing their effectiveness and return on investment.

Budget Management: Efficiently managing your campaign budgets is crucial for achieving cost-effective advertising. Set a realistic budget that aligns with your business goals and monitor its performance closely. Regularly review the allocation of your budget across campaigns and adjust as needed based on their performance. It's important to strike a balance between maximizing exposure and conversions while staying within your budget limits.

By implementing these key points from this book "The Essential Google Ads Guide", you'll be well-equipped to create and optimize successful Google Ads campaigns that drive relevant traffic, increase brand visibility, and generate valuable conversions for your business.

Remember to continually analyze and refine your strategies based on data insights to ensure the best possible results for your advertising efforts.

www.ingramcontent.com/pod-product-compliance
Lightning Source LLC
Chambersburg PA
CBHW080544220526

45466CB00010B/3032